A JOHN CATT PUBLICATION

WHY
TEACH?

BEN NEWMARK

First Published 2019

by John Catt Educational Ltd,
15 Riduna Park, Station Road,
Melton, Woodbridge IP12 1QT

Tel: +44 (0) 1394 389850
Email: enquiries@johncatt.com
Website: www.johncatt.com

ISBN: 978 1 912906 33 8

Set and designed by John Catt Educational Limited

Contents

Dedication:

To Bessie, for teaching me what education is really for; to Amber for holding everything together; and to everyone at the Nuneaton Academy for so quickly adopting me as part of the family.

How to read this book

I didn't realise that teaching was such a strange job until I'd been doing it for quite a while. Before becoming a teacher I'd been a late night bar supervisor and short order chef, which were equally bizarre ways to earn a living. It was not immediately clear to me how peculiar teaching was because I had little else to compare it with.

At the start of my career, young and trusting, I assumed that all the things I was told to do – from how to teach to how to record the progress of my pupils – were well planned and necessary. Sometimes things didn't feel right and seemed bizarre but, for the first couple of years of my career, I assumed this was because I was not skilled or knowledgeable enough to understand. I blindly followed orders, hoping they'd make sense as I became more experienced.

The feeling that things were not quite as well thought out as I had first thought began to grow through encounters with experienced teachers who were just as baffled as I was. Initially, to my shame, I scoffed at their confusion and objections without engaging with them. I assumed their views were out of date and not worth the bother of thinking about.

But I couldn't keep this up forever. Many of the confused experienced teachers were inspiring. I admired them. When they gave me advice it was helpful, even (perhaps especially) when it contradicted the school's party line or what my training had told me. When they raised concerns, I saw they were right more and more often.

So I began to ask questions, which led to answers which led to more questions. The more I learned the more confused I became.

To my horror it became clear that there was no master plan. There was no sense to much of what I saw around me at all. Instead, education was a world full of contradictory thinking, bad planning and unintended consequences.

Each chapter of this book tries to answer one of the questions I struggled with. I have tried to explain the reasons for the oddness and then give some advice on how schools and individual teachers might manage it.

And it is possible to do better than manage it. For all its weirdness there isn't another job in the world I'd rather do. When finally I have to retire, I'm pretty sure I'll be begging my closest school to let me teach two or three classes a week.

If I could afford to, I'd do it for free.

I hope this short book will help those confused by the many oddities of teaching get to the point I'm at now faster than I did. It's for those who find themselves baffled, and want to know why things are as they are. It's for those who want to work out how to navigate the twisting mazes and halls of mirrors, and have ambitions loftier than survival.

The chapters do not need to be read in any particular order, although I'd suggest leaving 'Why Teach?' until last.

Thank you for reading, and good luck. Despite its frustrations, teaching remains a noble, fulfilling and worthwhile thing to do with a life.

Why doesn't my school's behaviour system work?

Taylor, that's a warning. I'm putting your name on the board. Jamal, I know you talked while I was writing Taylor's warning on the board so your name is going on the board too. Yes, Jamal, I know Stacey talked too so I'll write her name on the board beneath yours. Stacey, that's a C2 for swearing at Jamal for telling me you talked. Phillipa, I know that swearing is a C3 but I'm the teacher so I decide. Yes, Taylor, I agree everyone is talking now. Class, you are all on a warning now and Taylor, Jamal and Stacey you are now all on a C2. Martha, stop arguing with me or you'll get a detention. Right, Martha you have a detention and I'm writing up a C4 on the board for you now. Shut up, everyone. I know she didn't get a warning but she shouldn't have argued. Anyone who talks from now on gets a detention. Right, that's it – whole-class detention after school tomorrow. Anyone who doesn't come will get two hours.

This is not supposed to happen. The whole point of school behaviour strategies is to avoid scenes like this one. One of the first documents given to new staff, they usually seem sensible and clear, and are reassuring to less experienced teachers understandably anxious about bad behaviour. Typically they offer a hierarchy of rewards and sanctions which, if followed consistently, should create a smooth, stress-free classroom in which learning flourishes.

Unfortunately they very often deliver far less than they promise and an inexperienced teacher can find that using their school's system causes more problems than it solves. On asking for help they are often told the system is sound and any issue is in their implementation: common criticisms are that not enough positive points are being handed out, or that they are issuing too many sanctions. New and nearly new teachers, who lack the experience to question what they are taught by more senior colleagues, believe this and spend a huge amount of time and energy trying to become fully compliant with their school's policy. If the policy is indeed robust, this can work; but if, as is often the case, the policy in itself is actually defective then such changes to practice just lead to further inconsistency and disruption. In the first part of this chapter I would like to discuss why so many apparently sensible and well-thought-out positive behaviour policies are actually inherently flawed before going on to what teachers can do when they find themselves working in places with ineffective strategies.

Why doesn't my school's positive behaviour strategy work?

Before working out why any strategy might not be working it is first fair to make sure the problem is definitely with the system and not you. Some clear indicators that the problem might lie close to home would be that everyone else in the school is using it faithfully, and that levels of reward and sanction are pretty consistent between teachers. It might also be worth checking that you are issuing the higher sanctions (e.g. detentions), as often solid systems fall apart if children learn their teacher is reluctant, for whatever reason, to hand these out when behaviour clearly warrants it. In schools where behaviour systems operate effectively, senior leadership probably will not be concerned about the number of sanctions you issue and will not aggressively question you over why you thought these necessary.

If you discover that, by and large, your colleagues are using the school system and have no complaints about it, then you should face the possibility you could be the weak link in the chain and even a reason others are struggling to apply it. Teachers who are not following the system because they do not know how, or are scared to do so, should ask for help. Those who don't follow the system because they are ideologically opposed to its principles should bring this up openly and may wish to move jobs if differences are not professionally reconcilable. Those teachers who choose not to follow strong systems because the force of their personalities, seniority of position or the length of their tenure at the school do their colleagues a disservice. By refusing to follow a sensible system, those that feel they do not need it undermine and weaken it for everyone else; if children never get detentions from a popular teacher for an infringement that deserves one, they will judge a teacher who gives them one as unjust and will argue, and this is unfair.

It is not surprising that SLTs claim any disciplinary problems in their schools are the result of poor implementation of a good system. Admitting otherwise means admitting bad policy, which calls into question the competence of general leadership and management. This is why school leadership is unlikely to accept criticism of the school's behaviour policy. It is far easier to blame those lower down the hierarchy for not doing it right than it is to accept that there are problems with what teachers are being asked to do in the first place. This issue is compounded by the fact children are far more likely to comply with a policy if it is being implemented by a senior member of staff with the clout to make their life immediately unpleasant. This makes it easy for SLT to believe the system is effective and that any problems must be down to failure to apply it properly. Less senior staff are also unlikely to admit (at least publicly) that they think the strategy is flawed because this can be taken as open criticism of their managers, which might cause them professional problems. More common is to pay lip service to the strategy while quietly muddling along alone and using individual approaches to varying degrees of success. If levels of reward and sanction vary wildly between different teachers, or the least well-behaved children seem to be accumulating very high proportions of rewards, it is likely that the school's strategy is not really working and may well be conceptually flawed for one or more of the following reasons.

1. The strategy is not as clear as it seems.

While a strategy may seem clear on paper, practice often reveals it to be far more ambiguous than it first appears. For example, a school's strategy may say that a pupil receives a first warning for 'Not listening to class instructions'. On the face of it, this is logical. A teacher is explaining a task and if a child is not listening properly, they issue a warning. The child then listens to the instructions. All is well.

Those with any familiarity with the inside of a classroom will probably already have spotted the issues here. How do we know if the child was listening or not? Gazing out of the window does not mean a child isn't listening. Nor does rummaging in a pencil case or walking to the bin to sharpen a pencil. So how do we prove the child was not listening if, as they may do, they argue back? Already, at the very lowest level, the apparently clear system is beginning to come undone.

An example of a higher-level infraction demanding a proportionally more severe response might be 'speaking in a disrespectful way to another child'. Here, problems with interpretation are likely to make this apparently sensible rule a nightmare to enforce. Is the good-natured ribbing of a friend by calling him an idiot for dropping his pen a 'disrespectful act' worthy of a sanction? What about if a one girl calls her neighbour a 'retard' and her neighbour says she doesn't mind? What about shouting 'retard' out of the window at a boy with cerebral palsy as he leaves another classroom early for his lunch? Does that warrant just a second-level sanction for a 'disrespectful act'? We may well have a very clear view on all of these, but this view might not be shared with our pupils; and even when it is, children can be extremely skilled at manipulating this apparent ambiguity to their own advantage by arguing their teacher has made a mistake interpreting the rule. Furthermore, no strategy can ever possibly include all misdeeds (although attempting to write one that does could be a lot of fun), which further adds to a sense of uncertainty and confusion when infringements not explicitly identified on the policy occur.

Teachers who find themselves agonising over their school's behaviour strategy poster or document trying to decide whether or not something deserved a C2 or a C3 are almost certainly wasting their time. The problem is most likely with the system.

2. Strategies are written under the assumption that pupils will accept the sanctions they are given.

When a school behaviour strategy is working properly, children do not argue back. If children are disputing sanctions in a lesson, it means there is a chance it will be overturned, or that a further sanction for arguing is not enough of a disincentive. School behaviour strategies always assume that incidents of bad behaviour happen in the context of order and that children will accept their teacher's decision. If this isn't actually the case then trying to apply the strategy can cause complete chaos: constant arguing causes so many further infringements that dealing with them becomes impossible and any semblance of order collapses under the sheer volume of disruption. In such environments, where teachers feel they have to justify their decisions, this to-and-fro undermines credibility and encourages children to see elements of the policy as negotiable. School behaviour strategies can only ever keep order; they cannot create it in the first place. If a school tolerates a culture of generally bad conduct, no classroom strategy will make behaviour better – and to say otherwise is disingenuous and unfair.

3. Nobody monitors the consistency of rewards and sanctions.

In some schools, while raw numbers of rewards and sanctions may be recorded and perhaps even analysed for patterns, little attention is paid to what they are given for. One teacher may issue a merit for completing all the work they set, while another may not because they regard this as a basic expectation undeserving of special reward. Similarly, one teacher may prefer to deal with shouting out by giving reminders or warnings, while another may immediately issue a demerit and associated detention for the same offence. While the inconsistency may be partly the result of vague language that allows multiple interpretations of the same act, this can still happen even when policy is sufficiently explicit if leadership takes a laissez-faire attitude towards how their teachers actually apply it. If schools place importance on only the numbers of rewards and sanctions and not what these are being given for, the inconsistency will cause any whole-school behaviour system to fragment with each teacher effectively working alone. In such instances it would actually be better if schools didn't bother with a pretence of a holistic approach at all, because the visible failure to enforce any uniformity undermines the perceived competence of the school as a whole.

4. Behaviour is viewed as a symptom of teaching quality.

Some of the schools which don't monitor why teachers issue rewards and sanctions instead place emphasis on the numbers of each handed out. It is quite common for the number of reward points to be read out publicly in briefings with departments and the individual teachers who give out the most being praised and those who hand out fewer shamed by association. This sort of foolishness, in addition to being infantile and unprofessional, is enormously damaging because it creates the impression that good teachers give lots of reward points and bad ones do not, which can make issuing them an end in itself. This impression is reinforced by schools in which teachers issuing comparatively high numbers of sanctions are asked to reduce this regardless of what these sanctions are issued for, leading to teachers becoming reluctant to punish pupils who deserve it because of the effect this will have on the way in which they are regarded by their colleagues and leadership. In such environments, teachers feel encouraged to hand out lots of rewards, deserved or not, because they feel this is a good way of proving their competence. This creates an arms race in which teachers have to award more and more to outperform each other. The effect of this hyperinflation – well explained by Doug Lemov in 'throwing scholar dollars' in his *Teach Like A Champion* blog (Lemov, 2015) – is the devaluation of the rewards altogether. This may well also help explain why it is common for a school's most disruptive pupils to receive comparatively high proportions of rewards; if a good teacher gives lots of rewards, what could be stronger evidence of competence than giving them to typically badly behaved children?

Another sign that behaviour is viewed as an output of the quality of teaching is when a school emphasises engagement or even enjoyment for its own sake. When this happens, poor behaviour, rather than being blamed on problems with the policy or choices made by children, is attributed to the failure of teachers to adequately keep and retain the attention of their pupils. Schools that believe this while operating positive behaviour strategies are, at best, conflicted: if poor conduct can be even partly explained by the standard of teaching, it is a very small step to excusing it for the same reason, which makes the consistent application of any system an irrelevance.

Teachers working in cultures like this often become afraid to log sanctions because they know this reflects badly on them, and that they may not be supported in applying them because they are more likely to be regarded as at fault than the child is.

When this happens, the result is (at best) the erosion or (at worst) the total destruction of the system's credibility.

Leaders that allow this to happen are not taking responsibility for the behaviour of children in their schools. It would be more honest (and fairer on everyone) to just say they see managing behaviour as the job of individual teachers and drop any pretence of a whole-school system. This would at least allow teachers more agency and eliminate some meaningless, time-sapping bureaucracy.

There is no halfway house: either there is a policy that everyone follows or there isn't one at all and it is every teacher for themselves.

5. The administrative burden of following up on sanctions is so overwhelming and demoralising, teachers don't do it.

In some schools the logging and implementation of sanctions is so byzantine that it seems intentional. Just finding a pupil on the school's database and entering a description of an incident – which can very much feel like a justification for punishment – can take a few minutes. This doesn't sound a lot but when, say, five pupils have misbehaved, the time soon adds up. If even three pupils misbehave in five lessons, the time spent entering the incidents is enough to be off-putting, especially if there is no certainty that this will have any effect. It is also worth noting what a demoralising and unpleasant task this is, made even less attractive if the teacher feels there is a chance they will be judged for a perceived inability to control the pupils involved.

Following up on an incident often only begins with logging it. Teachers in many schools are expected to run their own detentions, which requires them to give up their own time, which affects energy levels and morale. If (as is often the case) children choose not to attend a detention, the cycle begins again, with the teacher expected to log the failure to attend as a whole new incident. It is very common for some pupils to build up so many sanctions, even for comparatively low-level offenses, that there is simply not enough time for them to ever clear their backlog. This can happen especially quickly in schools which direct teachers to meetings or training or to teach interventions after school because there simply aren't enough slots to run detentions in. Senior leaders, perhaps understandably at a loss as to what to do, can end up downgrading sanctions, sometimes using the teacher's failure to adhere to prescriptive and exhaustive checklists as an excuse.

For example, if a policy says that teachers are expected to write to parents to tell them about a missed detention before setting another and they do not do this – or do but forget to log a record that they have – the sanction may be postponed or even cancelled. Finally, very big backlogs may be cancelled at the end of term in order to give whole groups of children 'a fresh start'.

Following procedure can very quickly become an end in itself. Teachers may be told, for example, that before a certain sanction can be considered they must make a phone call home and log it, regardless of how many times that year the parents have been called already, and regardless of how ineffective this has been up to that point.

In such schools, a general lethargy often emerges and new appointees can be utterly baffled by unwritten rules that may directly contradict those on the official policy. A school rule may say clearly that any swearing results in an automatic detention but those who have been at the school for any length of time may know this is never applied and that any teacher who tries is viewed as a pedantic jobsworth.

Teachers working in schools like this can be forgiven for becoming so exhausted and demoralised that they stop issuing or logging sanctions at all. It is possible that in some schools this isn't challenged because nobody wants to challenge the pleasant narrative that behaviour is improving – whether or not this is really true. Intentional or not, the result is the same. It does not take children long to work out that the policy displayed on the posters in their classrooms is a fiction. Some will resent this because they see their classmates getting away with murder and spoiling things for them. Others will have enormous fun taking full advantage.

6. Strong teachers and those with more influence choose not to use the system.

Even when a school's behaviour policy is sensible in principle it can still fail. If a behaviour policy is to work properly, everyone must use it. In some schools, stronger teachers, or those with more influence such as members of SLT, do not use the system because they feel they do not need to. This is understandable; if a teacher can teach well without using a superfluous layer of bureaucracy, why not let them? This, theoretically, saves time and allows more autonomy for those who have earned it.

The problem here is how it affects the way in which teachers are seen by their pupils. If the strongest, most senior teachers do not use the policy, teachers who do are perceived as weaker and less important by association. This can easily lead to children behaving very differently depending on who is teaching them. This effect is compounded when punishments vary according to the relative status of teachers in the school hierarchy. When this happens, behaviour will be more the result of complex and variable power dynamics than it will be the result of consistency within a planned system. In an unfortunate and cruel irony, this also means that those least equipped to deal with bad behaviour (for example, NQTs and supply teachers) tend to be those most often subjected to it.

It is deeply unfair and unhelpful to ascribe a member of staff's struggles with pupil behaviour to their failure to implement the policy if the school's most respected teachers are not doing so.

7. High-level sanctions, even when they are explicit on the policy, are very rarely applied.

Most school behaviour policies have permanent exclusion as the ultimate, final sanction. This is typically for an extreme incident affecting the safety and security of the school, or for many lower-level incidents. In schools without an effective behaviour policy, it is rare for a child to be excluded for less serious incidents regardless of how many of these there are. Some schools (unwisely, if they lack the will or ability to follow through) place an actual figure on the number of behaviour points that should result in a permanent exclusion. While reaching this should result in the end of the road for the pupil concerned, more common is a sequence of meetings and contracts in which the child is given one of many 'final' warnings. The effect of this, on both the child concerned and their compatriots, is to make a mockery of the policy and the school by association. Lion-taming only works if the animals can be convinced that their keepers are more dangerous than they really are. If this illusion is shattered, the keepers find themselves in great danger. The same is true of threatening children with sanctions that cannot be enforced: once pupils realise the school is effectively powerless, they become unaccountable to anyone but themselves. If they have high standards of personal behaviour, this is unlikely to have really serious consequences; but if they do not, the consequences can be very severe indeed.

8. So many children end up with sanctions that they become normalised and stop being a disincentive.

A common strategy adopted by schools who wish to signal they are getting tough on behaviour is to introduce a strict new set of rules and then issue all pupils in breach of these rules with a planned sanction. For example, a school may decide on a new uniform and place all children who refuse to wear it in isolation, or even send them home. Or, a school may decide to be more vigilant on homework and assign children who do not do it a detention for each unfinished piece. In the short term, this may result in a very high number of children being sanctioned, which can place a school's administrative capacity under great strain. In itself, there is nothing wrong with this; and if such deterrents work in reducing the undesirable behaviour then (unless they are in some way unethical) they may be worth the effort required to implement them. Problems only occur if the number of sanctions never declines – because when this happens, in addition to the problems caused by the extra workload, sanctions are normalised and cease to be a meaningful disincentive. This is even more likely to happen when pupils think sanctions are unfair or pointless. For example, if a school is issuing detentions for not completing homework, but does nothing about the many pupils who just copy work in order to avoid the sanction, the system will lack the credibility required to be accepted as necessary.

It is even possible for children to develop learned helplessness as they come to believe sanctions are handed out randomly and that they have no control over whether they are punished or not. This fatalism is incompatible with the sense of responsibility and agency pupils need in order to be inspired into making good choices – and dooms policies to failure.

9. Allowances are made for some children and the reasons for these allowances are not understood or accepted by others.

The degree to which school behaviour strategies should be no-excuses policies is one of the most controversial questions in education and this isn't the right place to get into the debate. It's enough to say that any exceptions to the general rule, if there are any, should indeed be exceptional. If they are not, and lots of children visibly break rules without consequence while other children are punished for the same acts, pupils will perceive the system as unfair and will not respect it.

This can affect teachers just as much. A school may, rightly or wrongly, ascribe specific special educational needs to some pupils. For example, a child may be diagnosed as having behavioural or emotional difficulties which require time outside the classroom to calm down after being given a sanction. If teachers agree this is necessary then they will apply this alteration to the general policy diligently; but if they believe the diagnosis to be unsafe or just an excuse for deliberately making poor choices, their irritation in having to do so is likely to affect their implementation.

An effective behaviour policy which allows exceptions requires that children and teachers understand there are good reasons for these, and to have faith they are necessary even when confidentiality agreements mean there isn't an explanation. This is a difficult culture to create, but those schools that fail to do so risk resentment and subversion.

What to do

Schools with effective and cohesive behaviour strategies can be found in all types of area. The underlying reason they are effective is that the school genuinely believes its children are capable of behaving well. When a school lacks this belief, for whatever reason, any system will fail because those responsible for upholding it feel they have no choice but to make unofficial ad hoc adjustments.

Working out whether or not a school has a working behaviour policy is comparatively easy. Before applying for a job, ask for a copy of the school's policy and visit the school to observe some lessons. Don't just look for good behaviour as this could be the result of a particular teacher, but instead look to see how closely the teachers you observe are using the policy. If they are not following it closely, it is likely the system isn't used; if they are using it, the chances are the system is effective.

The lack of a functioning policy is not necessarily a reason not to apply to a school. In some areas, particularly those in which children are taught to behave appropriately at home, schools can get by quite well without one because the children in it already have high standards of personal behaviour. However, in more challenging contexts, the lack of a working policy can be a source of enormous unhappiness – particularly if blame for the ensuing bad behaviour is placed on teachers. From a purely teacher-centred perspective, schools like this are best avoided it if can be helped.

That said, even in the most challenging of contexts it is possible, albeit extremely difficult, to create an orderly and purposeful classroom without a functioning whole-school behaviour policy. However, before giving any suggestions on how to do this it is very important to be honest and open about the risks inherent in attempting to do so.

It is difficult for anyone who has never experienced what it is like to teach in a school in which poor behaviour is the norm to appreciate just how bad it can get. When there is no respect for authority, children can be shockingly rude and hurtful to both each other and their teachers. When this happens, it is difficult for even the most stable, balanced and naturally patient person to remain calm and act in a reasoned fashion. Working day to day in such environments can cause misery and damage health. It is also possible for teachers to be pushed so hard – even if this is just down to the steady drip-drip of day-in-day-out disobedience – that they react in unprofessional ways, or are accused of such behaviour (even when it is not true) by children who have no respect for the adults responsible for them. This has ended the careers of some teachers; and even when it doesn't, the effects can be truly awful.

If teachers do nothing else to prepare for working in such a school, they should make sure they are a member of a union.

Teachers who do go into such schools should do so with their eyes open. It is very easy, driven by the same idealism used to recruit teachers into the profession, to make naive choices based on inaccurate assumptions and deeply regret it later, sometimes to the extent of leaving teaching altogether. These are significant losses at a time when teachers are scarcer than they have been for years.

For teachers already working in such environments and unwilling or unable to move, or for those who accept the risks in working at challenging schools with non-functional behaviour systems but nonetheless feel compelled to stay, the following suggestions might be helpful. Before implementing any of them, it is important to be sure that the school's system is beyond redemption. Teachers working with a good behaviour policy and the support of their colleagues and SLT are lucky, and they should not undermine it by going alone even if it has no negative repercussions for them personally. It is easy to build affection and respect with pupils in the short term by ignoring policy and revelling in a sort of rebel status. But to do so is a failure of professional duty because it is an implied criticism of those who do faithfully follow the policy. Even if a system is dysfunctional it would be unprofessional to act independently unless concerns have been shared with leadership, who have a right to respond. Ideally, such a conversation would be the starting point for the establishment of a working policy. Only when this has been done and concerns have been dismissed or ignored should teachers consider taking matters into their own hands. Even then, ideally, teachers should not be clandestine: they should be open about what they do in their classroom if asked.

Teachers in this position might begin by accepting they will need to create a tight classroom system that, as much as is possible in their context, avoids the mistakes discussed in the first section of this chapter. Although this is always tough, it is usually easier if you are new to the group. If you are not and are trying to turn round an existing negative climate then be explicit with the class that this is what you are doing because their behaviour is too poor for them to learn anything.

Introducing a long list of rules and expectations is usually a mistake because it may overload children, who may also be so used to this sort of thing that they won't take any notice. Better is to introduce a limited number of clear high-leverage rules (for example, 'Nobody talks when I do'), explain the reason for them ('Because you're here to learn and if you talk while I do, you won't), and then focus on these. Once these have been embedded, more rules can be gradually introduced. If children fail to even try to respect the first rules, it might be wise to enlist the help of another teacher the class respect to help communicate and enforce these rules in the early stages. If you do choose to do this, make it clear to the class that the extra member of staff is present by your considered and measured invitation – you want to avoid making it look like you have 'called Daddy' because you can't cope.

Consequences for breaking any rule should be clear and the same every time. For example, 'I'll give a three-second count every time I want to speak. If you talk after this, you get 10 minutes after school. If you do it twice, 20 minutes.' Giving pupils 'warnings' is often counterproductive – especially in environments in which children are used to breaking rules with relative impunity – and really shouldn't be necessary if rules and consequences have been clearly explained.

Teachers doing this should be emotionally and logistically prepared for a great deal of kickback in the early stages. If you know that you are going to have to focus on turning behaviour around, make this intentional and do not worry too much about not getting through any specified amount of content. Remember that if a class isn't concentrating properly, merely superficially skimming through some basic tasks does not mean anything has been learned. Classes may well break any new rules en masse in order to try to overload your system. It is absolutely imperative that no matter what the provocation, you do not compromise or lose your temper. Children in chaotic schools are used to this and will think they have broken you. Instead, remain calm and make a note of every child who breaks a rule and how many times they did without making a scene of doing so. At this stage, it may even be wise to ignore other offences other than your priorities (unless, of course, they are dangerous). Remember that, although children may say really hurtful things, this behaviour is not personal; it is an attack on authority and your position as a teacher in general.

Then, after the lesson, follow up.

This will be logistically difficult and emotionally exhausting, certainly in the early stages. It is best to accept and plan for this. Eat well, get enough sleep and exercise. As tempting as it might be to unwind with a drink in the evenings, be aware of the emotional effect alcohol may have on you and never go to school hungover. Being on edge, for whatever reason, will make it much harder to respond consistently and purposefully to behavioural challenges. Avoid talking about what is going on at school too much once you leave the building. While venting can feel like it's doing some good at the time, it actually makes it harder to unwind.

Above all else – marking, planning, making resources or whatever – do absolutely everything in your power to make sure that sanctions you decided on are implemented for every child. Use form tutors, heads of department and heads of year. Phone home. Ask form tutors, heads of department and heads of year to phone home too. Make sure the focus of all communications is on the logistics of applying your sanction and not the reasons for the bad behaviour. Do not justify decisions you have made beyond what you told the child and, at all costs, avoid getting into blow-by-blow post-mortems from which you will only emerge weaker. You will in all likelihood not be able to get every child to accept sanctions immediately, but you don't actually need to. If you can create a critical mass of compliance, then those refusing become marginalised and, while they may still be problematic in your lessons, it will be much more difficult for them to suck others into misbehaviour. This is not, of course, an ideal situation; but in schools without functioning behaviour systems, it might be the best you can achieve – and certainly an improvement.

Do not fall into the trap, especially in the early stages, of making detentions impromptu restorative justice sessions, or using them as opportunities to build relationships through informal chat. They should be punishments. A 15-minute silent detention is much more effective than an hour that feels like a youth club and runs the risk of undermining your authority. If the child refuses to comply with the conditions of a detention by, for example, arguing with you in it, then send them home and chase up the next day. Whatever is said, remain calm and show confidence – even when you don't have it – that in the end, the child will have to comply.

In lessons, do not bring up outstanding sanctions, refuse to discuss them, and treat each as a fresh start with the same rules you always have. If a child refuses to accept a sanction by, for example, telling you explicitly that 'I never do detentions and I'm not going to do this one', then tell a superior and suggest the child be excluded from your lessons until they have completed your sanction. If they are reluctant to give you permission to do this, ask politely for alternative suggestions and word objections as questions rather than statements. Use inclusive language to make it clear you regard yourself as part of a team by, for example, saying 'If we let Curtis back in when he's told other children he won't do my detention, what will the rest of the class think?'

Your efforts are more likely to be successful if you can convince others in your department, corridor or block to agree to adopt your approach too. Even buddying up with the teacher of a completely different subject in a different area of the school can help if you teach the same children. While all teachers doing the same thing is the ideal, even a few can help create a feeling of consistency. If you decide to do this, be explicit about it to your classes so they know what is coming. Say something like 'You're going to notice that Mrs Turner and I are doing things the same way from now on.'

Sadly, all this effort does not guarantee success; and at some point there remains little alternative but to accept defeat. Factors outside a teacher's control – including school philosophy and policy, class changes and wider staff turnover – can all doom the most careful plan to failure. Personal circumstances can also have an impact. Going it alone when the environment is not conducive can be both physically and emotionally exhausting; and issues at home, such as a new baby or relationship difficulties, can make it just too much. If, for whatever reason, it becomes clear that there has been no improvement, it is better to be proud that you tried and look for work elsewhere. Not doing so can, even to the most positive of people, lead to a loss of faith that certain groups of children can behave well at all, along with a general lowering of expectations. This pernicious and enormously damaging belief can be very hard to shift once it has got hold.

There is no shame in leaving an impossible situation and no medals for martyring yourself. Teachers aren't social workers, prison guards, firefighters, nightclub bouncers, entertainers or police officers, and those that find they have to play one of these roles regularly in their work should not be judged for making the professional decision to move to a place where they can just do their job. There are plenty of schools in which children behave well and it is perfectly reasonable to want to teach in one.

Why am I told such different things about how to improve my teaching?

After the last round of observations at my school I was told my teaching was not good enough and placed on a support plan. Although everyone involved – and there's a lot of people involved – tells me this is to help me and my pupils, it has also been made clear that if there isn't improvement this could ultimately result in formal capability procedures. While I recognise things could be better, and I do want to improve, I'm really confused because everyone is giving me such different advice. An external consultant tells me I should give my pupils more freedom and let them work more in groups; but my in-school coach says I should be stricter and rearrange the desks in my room into rows. My head of department wants my pupils to do more essay writing, but the assistant headteacher in charge of teaching and learning thinks my lessons don't give the children enough opportunity to be creative or to develop their growth mindsets. Following the recommendations of one person seems to mean going against the recommendations of another. I am getting more and more anxious and this is affecting my confidence.

Regrettably this is a common issue in schools, where even teachers regarded as doing a good job can find themselves buffeted by contradictory pedagogical advice. For experienced teachers, confident in their own style and given the autonomy to teach how they see fit, it is easier to know which suggestions are worth listening to and which are not. For those subjected to intensive intervention – whether this is because of an underlying culture of distrust, lack of experience or questions around competency – it can be much harder.

When (for whatever reason) schools expect a teacher to improve, they usually introduce a large volume of support drawn from those regarded as strong practitioners. While this support is often described as voluntary (in the early stages at least), those offered it understand that should they choose to turn any of it down, this will be formally recorded and reflect very badly on the individual concerned if teaching does not get better. Indeed, with improvement often highly subjective, a perceived unwillingness to engage with support could actually contribute to an impression that teaching standards are stagnant even when there has been progress.

This would not be such an issue if support was always helpful and consistent, but often it is not. When support lacks an overall direction the result is often a contradictory cacophony of ideas, philosophy and methods which confuses teachers and pupils. Lurching between very different approaches can actually make things even worse than they had been before 'help' began because it means the teacher never gets the chance to get better at anything and looks disorganised and uncertain to their pupils, which leads to even greater disruption. For example, a teacher who spends one week trying to teach didactically from the front and the next facilitating group work is likely to spend most of their time and energy resolving logistical issues, making teaching inevitably ineffective. This can place a struggling teacher in a hole they simply cannot get out of, as measures supposed to help them actually end up making things worse, further reinforcing the impression that they are weak and inviting progressively more aggressive intervention.

One reason this happens is that there is no consensus within the profession about what schools are for. In effect, there are multiple, often mutually exclusive answers because there isn't agreement on what we are trying to achieve. Some believe the purpose of schools to be preparation for future employment or even for hypothetical jobs that may exist in the future. These people may be more likely to advocate methods that promote supposedly transferable skills such as teamwork or communication and to be in favour of working in groups and using technology. Others feel that the quality of a school can be best measured by the grades achieved by its pupils. These may want to see the regular use of mark schemes and sample exam responses. Or, a teacher may believe the purpose of education is to pass down 'the best of what has been thought and said', and advocate traditional direct teaching and the seating of children in rows. If teachers of such radically different philosophies are all involved in the support of someone struggling, it should really not surprise anybody that the end result is so confusing.

Although they may be unaware of it, simply choosing activities for children to do makes teachers part of an ancient philosophical debate which has run through English schools for as long as they have existed. From the 1970s until quite recently educational progressivism has had the upper hand in many state schools. This was interpreted to mean that education should be child centred, with lessons built around the interests and developmental stages of the individual children in them. It was generally assumed that children who behaved badly or failed to complete work did so either because they were demonstrating needs that needed to be addressed, or because the content of their lessons was not relevant or engaging. This put the onus on schools and teachers to make adjustments, with less emphasis on teaching pupils to feel personal responsibility for their work ethic and actions. Teaching the whole class for extended periods of time became frowned upon in many contexts, because what was perceived to be a 'one-size-fits-all' approach was not compatible with the prevailing belief that content needed to be adapted to the different needs of individuals. Instead of a 'sage on a stage', teachers were often expected to be 'a guide on the side', facilitating bespoke learning journeys instead of trying to take all members of the class to the same destination.

While this was exhausting and ineffective for many teachers, it did provide clarity for those comfortable with unquestioningly following orders. Between the early and mid 2000s, English schools, influenced by the way in which Ofsted inspected and reported, typically took a confident ideological stance: good teaching meant being child centred, which brought with it a wave of associated policy. While Ofsted has claimed, and will continue to claim, they have never communicated a preference for any teaching style, reports from this era often praised the practice of schools who adopted progressive practice, encouraging others to do the same, and discouraging more didactic, traditional approaches (Old, 2013). This claim looks particularly suspect given that Chief Inspector Christine Gilbert blamed boring teachers for poor behaviour of pupils in 2009 (Curtis, 2009).

Whether right or wrong to do so, teachers felt they had no choice but to fall in line with this philosophy or ship out, and some teachers who refused to adapt their more traditional styles feel this ended their careers. This was further reinforced by much teacher training (both ITT and CPD) which presented this as the accepted and unchallenged best way to teach. It was in this environment that many people leading schools today were trained, which helps explain why many schools still seem to have a lingering preference for it. If this had definitely delivered improved results, teachers would probably still be forced to teach this way; but it did not. While saying that this style of teaching is always ineffective in every instance might be going too far, PISA results (Ashman, 2017) and recent research supporting the efficacy of more traditional, explicit, didactic instruction have ended the hegemony of child-centred learning.

At a time when a firm hand on the rudder would be more useful than ever, Ofsted has, until very recently, been silent on what exactly constitutes good teaching. This timidity, while historically uncharacteristic, makes perfect sense. Rightly criticised for wrongly endorsing a specific pedagogical style in the past, its own credibility seriously knocked by the mistakes it made in doing so, Ofsted absented itself from the debate. Preferring to sit on the sidelines, it limited itself to checking how consistently teachers follow policies set by their schools, while resolutely refusing to take a view on whether or not these policies were sensible. Recently, under new Chief Inspector of Schools Amanda Spielman, Ofsted appears to have re-entered the arena with its endorsement of knowledge-rich approaches. This is encouragingly research informed but it is, as yet in early 2019, far too soon to say what effect this is likely to have, especially given the considerable freedom afforded academies, free schools and multi-academy trusts – along with the embedded resistance from powerful educationalists, unions and other interest groups.

While the current state of play is an improvement on the recent past it has presented schools and teachers with new problems. Whereas once there was a party line there is now more and increasing room for diverse views, which has meant that the range of advice offered to teachers is wider than it has ever been. The waters have been further muddied because, so far, teachers and schools have struggled to effectively apply the findings of supposedly illuminating research in meaningful, sustained ways. To those properly engaged in academic research it is clear we are further away than ever from a clear consensus on what constitutes effective teaching. Difficulties in replicability and questions over research methods have meant that, even when the end objective is made explicit, highly regarded and high-profile researchers, such as Carol Dweck and John Hattie, have been very robustly critiqued (Didau, 2017a). If there is any pattern in the chaos it is that ideas rarely endure unchallenged for long and that there are never simple, clear solutions. It is just as reasonable to be concerned that those responsible for disseminating research to practising teachers may cherry-pick studies to reinforce their existing views.

All of this has made those responsible for the quality of teaching in schools directionless. For many – whether unaware of the debate or just thoroughly confused by it – a sort of everyday pragmatism seems to make the most sense. Unfortunately this typically manifests itself as what has worked for the individual providing support to a struggling teacher, which are invariably ideas and strategies formed, whether consciously or unconsciously, within the framework of their own ideology and subjective past experiences. Briefly, what teachers think is good advice for someone else is often what they feel 'works for me', which may be completely inappropriate for someone else even if we could prove (which we usually can't) that the strategy being suggested is effective in the first place. Further complicating this are the problems everyone has in assessing their own competence and expertise, and the role of confirmation bias when we make judgements about what is effective and what is not. Most of us have a tendency to overrate our own effectiveness when assessing our own performance – a phenomenon known as illusory superiority – and to explain away or ignore evidence that does not fit in with our existing world view. This means that while we may be predisposed to think we are more effective than a struggling teacher and in a position to help them, this may not actually be the case at all (Ghose, 2013). Even when those with supervisory responsibility over a struggling teacher feel their advice is based on empirical research, unless they are very regularly keeping up to date with developments in the field it is at least possible that some of what they suggest will be out of date.

Strong subject-specific ideas developed by expertise in disciplinary networks over a long period of time can act as a defence against new fads and provide helpful direction. For example, in history, the work of the Historical Association (and its journal, *Teaching History*) provides the organisation's members with a repository of disciplinary knowledge and an understanding of the controversies that have played out over many years, allowing teachers to position themselves within an established framework and be better aware of whether or not a shiny new idea is likely to be worth devoting time to or not. Even when these networks – in effect a discipline's collective memory – aren't available, support from experienced teachers within the same specialism as those they are helping is much more likely to be helpful than advice from someone outside the field, because they will have a better understanding of what the end result should look like and if the most important aspects of a given topic have been covered.

Sadly, this expertise and the direction it provides may be becoming increasingly rare. Expansions to SLT teams, attributed by Professor Becky Allen (2017) to increases in budgets during the New Labour years, have created a larger class of senior management. This, together with an increasingly young teacher demographic in many areas and a punishing pay cap which has resulted in a real-terms cut for all teachers, has normalised early promotion and eroded the status of both heads of department and classroom teachers. Now, those with the potential to be really strong subject specialists are often promoted into general roles before they have themselves fully grasped the unique demands of their own disciplines, and well before they have the opportunity to pass expertise along. The result of showing promise in subject-specific middle leadership can be immediate promotion out of it. This hollowing-out of subject-specific expertise has caused a rise in the belief that generic, one-size-fits-all approaches can benefit everyone.

While it is not impossible for non-subject specialists be helpful, particularly around areas such as classroom management and culture, it can be very difficult for them to see beyond what worked for them as a classroom teacher of a different subject. This means the advice they give is often disciplinarily inappropriate. For example, a drama teacher asked to support an English teacher may well end up recommending improvised roleplay; while an English teacher supporting a history teacher could push for creative writing. Whether or not these are authentic and worthwhile activities is unlikely to be of concern to the teacher providing support as they are unlikely to know, outside their own specialism, what is and what is not appropriate.

The result of all this is utter confusion as those who most need help find the advice they are given to be more a result of the individual preferences of the person giving it than it is anything else. Without certainty as to what good teaching is there will never be consensus; and given that disagreement over the purpose of schooling is inevitable, there can never be certainty. As a system we do not definitively know how to improve teaching, but with professional status and reputations dependent on saying the exact opposite, few are willing to admit it. So what we have is a proliferation of different philosophies, methods, strategies and styles, often existing in the same school, department and even within individual teachers. Many of these are contradictory, and expecting teachers to apply them all is a recipe for disaster. And yet, every day, we do.

It really is no wonder so many of us are so confused as to how to get better at teaching.

What to do

The single most helpful thing any confused teacher can do to get clarity is to familiarise themselves with the debate – preferably from within the context of their own subject – in order to gain a sense of the advantages and disadvantages of each philosophy, and then decide where they want to position themselves. There is little point trying to change anything without a particular end goal in mind. If we want to get better we must begin by being really clear about what exactly we want to get better at. Matthew Hood (Twitter: @matthewhood), the CEO of the Institute for Teaching, speaks a great deal of sense when he talks about intentionality. He means that the choices we make should be deliberate with the aim of eventually achieving a specific vision. Without this we are at the mercy of external factors and can find ourselves in a state of eternal bewilderment. Teachers need to know whether they want to work on improving their explanations, or to get better at facilitating group work, or at building pupil oracy, and why whatever they have chosen is a priority for them. This is not to say that all suggestions coming from divergent philosophies should be summarily dismissed, but it is important to know where priorities lie to avoid becoming distracted by the attempt to be all things to all people.

How easy this is to do depends on individual schools. Things are clearest when a school has an explicit educational philosophy, because this means individual preferences must be subordinate to institutional ones for the good of the community as a whole. For example, teachers choosing to work at Michaela Community School in London have a very clear traditional view on how they should teach and why, as do teachers at School 21 which has an equally clear (if radically different, more progressive) philosophy. Such clarity can be enormously helpful; teachers understand right from the application process what is expected and are free to seek employment elsewhere if they find the vision incompatible with their own. Things are trickier if a school is not explicit about its core purpose and methodology. While such places might defend themselves by saying they are pragmatic and just do whatever works, the lack of clear direction as to what this looks like means teachers who struggle in such places are far less likely to get coherent and consistent help.

Schools choosing to follow what they regard as a pragmatic, piecemeal approach to teaching and learning must be careful they do not implicitly favour one style over another if they want to avoid confusing and upsetting the teachers who work in them. Such schools might be wise to adopt a very clear position on 'hygiene' factors that mark lessons as either acceptable or unacceptable. For example it would be reasonable to say that, whichever style a teacher chooses to adopt, the lesson must be orderly and pupils must listen when their teacher is talking. But beyond this, schools should refrain from making a judgement on teaching because by doing so it is almost inevitable that criticisms end up being on stylistic choices rather than quality of application. Instead, lesson observations should aim to develop the teacher's own sense of self and intentionality by posing questions and encouraging reflection.

The lack of a unifying school vision on teaching and learning can be at least partially mitigated if the department in which a teacher works provides one. Teachers struggling in departments which have clear and explicit educational beliefs may be able to call on their immediate line management to broker support, ensuring that it is in line with a strong, shared philosophy. This, of course, relies on strong leadership and the ability of middle management to go to bat for struggling teachers when support is not helpful. Teachers fortunate enough to benefit from this should work collaboratively to develop support plans that are cohesive and over which they feel they have ownership.

Unfortunately, these scenarios are probably not typical. Many teachers are under pressure to urgently improve work in environments in which there is no meaningful educational ideology and are, like the teacher at the start of this chapter, subjected to inconsistent and incoherent advice and expected to follow it all. It is vital these teachers try to take control.

This does not mean all is lost. Teachers in this position could begin by openly sharing their own priorities. This is perhaps best done in writing, referencing academic work and showing this is the result of deep and serious thought. They should then clearly identify the sort of support they would like, ideally also saying who they would like to get this from – for example, writing, 'I would like to get help with building the listening skills of my pupils. I know Sally is really good at doing this so I'd like help from her.' It is also worthwhile, wherever possible, to try and source help from subject specialists. While dictating the sort of help you want might seem a frightening thing to do, it is important to remember that support plan meetings always ask teachers what help they would like as part of the process. And while cynicism is tempting (especially for those feeling under attack), it is professional to take the offer as genuine until proven otherwise. Indeed, it is quite likely that teachers doing this will find the approach welcomed, as it demonstrates proactivity and may well mean less work for those responsible for overseeing the plan.

If there is improvement, acknowledging and sharing it is a good idea as it creates the narrative that things are getting better, and increases your own confidence. Being positive about helpful support also makes it much easier to be honest when something isn't working. This should always be expressed politely with the acknowledgement that even when advice is misguided, those who give it have done so with good intentions and probably have spent their own time thinking about and giving it. Make any critique non-personal, for example, saying, 'I think Dan is outstanding and I really appreciate his work, but what he does so well isn't really what I'm working on at the moment. Could I focus on what I'm working on with Sally for the time being?'

While this approach may result in improvement and an easing of pressure, unfortunately it does not guarantee it. Even the most open and constructive approach can still fail.

If it does, it might be for one of two reasons.

Firstly, some schools feel they have the capacity to understand what a teacher needs to do to improve better than they do themselves and are unwilling to allow them to meaningfully contribute to the plan. In some cases, a school may indeed have a better idea of what an inexperienced teacher needs; but in others, this may be more to do with professional egos than a genuine understanding of what getting better means. Teachers who experience this can find themselves in an impossible position, as their confidence – a prerequisite of effective teaching – is eroded, spinning up into a vicious cycle. Teachers certain this is happening to them should try to leave as soon as they can. The insidious psychological effects of perceived continued underperformance and the relentless pressure that comes as a consequence can destroy careers even when the person on the receiving end is sure any fault isn't their own.

What might have been only a short-term blip can end up in anxiety, depression and lifelong scars.

The second reason a constructive approach to support procedures might not work is very unpleasant and, while comparatively rare, most teachers have probably seen it at least once. An unethical school or individual might, for whatever reason, judge it expedient that someone leave and then use support and competency mechanisms to force them out. Even if teachers in this situation do improve, this will be ignored because the end aim, whatever they do, is the termination of their employment. However those who do this sort of thing justify it to themselves, it is bullying and deeply immoral. Teachers who suspect this should find someone who they trust at the school and ask them outright if they think this is happening. It might also be wise to find out if the school or individual has a track record of this sort of behaviour as such incidents are rarely isolated.

Those that are sure the real aim of supposed support is to force them out have a difficult choice to make. In schools or areas with strong union presence it may well be worth fighting, especially if by doing so there is a chance of stopping the bullying happening to others in the future. This, however, is much easier to say than do when in the midst of the all-consuming horror of such a situation. Such bullying can be subtle, its perpetrators skilled in masking their true intentions; and a positive outcome is far from certain. Even winning such a case can end up as a defeat if those responsible stay in position and continue to have influence over their victim. Given all this, teachers choosing to resign before competency procedures (aware these must be disclosed to prospective future employers) may well be behaving entirely rationally and should not be judged. As a minimum, if teachers are to have any chance at getting better, however good they are to begin with, they must work in a place where there is belief they are capable of improvement and where there is a sincere desire to help them.

Those involved in bullying – whether it originates from them or whether they are complicit – should be ashamed of themselves. Not only does it push teachers out of the profession at the time we need them more than ever, it can also ruin lives.

Why are there so many spreadsheets in schools?

One of the reasons I became a teacher was that I didn't want to work in an office. The thought of spending my life in front of a computer screen poring over spreadsheets and databases filled me with dread. I was really excited by the idea of teaching children a subject I love and none of the recruitment adverts said anything about being a database and spreadsheet whizz. Nor did my training; we got lots of stuff on teaching and learning but weren't taught anything about analysing thousands of numbers. Now I'm in my first teaching job and finding the sheer number of spreadsheets intimidating and depressing. We have to log everything: attendance, behaviour, grades and lots of other stuff too. So much of my job seems to be learning how to interpret all the numbers, generating reports and sitting in meetings looking through spreadsheet after spreadsheet after report after report. Actual teaching – which I love just as much as I expected to – feels like a much smaller a part of my job than I thought it would be.

This problem is relatively new. Fifteen years ago, spreadsheets – at least in the form schools use them today – just didn't exist. Registers were paper based and schools didn't have the technological ability or inclination to collect or analyse as much data as they do now. The first change I remember was when the school I was working at bought in primitive tablets and gave one to each teacher. These were mini computers with monochromatic LCD displays on which we took registers. They also allowed teachers to wirelessly send each other short text messages, which was a feature sometimes used to communicate important information about pupils but more often used to arrange trips to the pub after work. I also heard that, although the school never got round to doing it before I left for a stint abroad, it was possible to place mark-sheets on the tablets so teachers would be able to see how their pupils were getting on in other lessons.

This, at the time, seemed quite exciting.

When I returned five years later things had changed. SIMS (School Information Management System), a computer program I had never heard of before leaving, now seemed to be at the centre of everything schools did. It was used to take the register for all lessons, and each half term a grade – GCSE at KS4 and based on old national curriculum levels at KS3 – was logged on a system by every teacher for every pupil they taught.

Reports, which I had handwritten before leaving the UK, had been replaced by generic comment banks on SIMS that teachers selected by pointing and clicking with a mouse.

All this data could be exported onto Excel and analysed, generating reports on individuals, whole cohorts and smaller groups, for example children who ate free school meals or those with special educational needs. Individual children could be compared to individual children, subjects could be compared against subjects, departments against other departments and teachers against teachers.

The possibilities were limitless.

This was a complicated business and to meet the new thirst for numbers a whole new order of roles had been created.

Most schools now have an assistant headteacher – or even a professional data manager – whose job it is to coordinate and track the numbers. Commercial, private companies who make the systems to collect and manage data have also helped drive the almost exponential increase in what is analysed – after all, selling upgrades to such software is how they make money. A symbiotic relationship between those in charge of data in schools and the companies that allow them to use it has created a cycle that continues to increase the amount of data that schools (and the teachers in them) are expected to collect and use.

More aggressive accountability has also led to the rise of the spreadsheet. When individual children, or groups of them, are not deemed to be learning fast enough, teachers are often expected to do extra tasks to try to close any gaps the spreadsheets say exist. These tasks, typically called interventions, must also be logged onto spreadsheets in order to assess the impact they have.

Spreadsheets now create more spreadsheets.

All this data has brought some undoubted benefits. For example, it is now possible to know instantly whether a pupil who should have turned up to school or a lesson actually has done, making our children better protected than they have ever been.

On the face of it, the data revolution also brought further, more subtle improvements.

It now appeared possible to track pupil progress and to hold teachers individually accountable for the learning of the pupils they taught. If a child was getting good grades in one subject but not in another, an apparently legitimate avenue of enquiry opened up. Even better, this line of enquiry was based not on the personal views of the teachers' line managers but on empirical numbers. This allowed school leaders to make decisions about who their high-performing departments and teachers were. The data was addictive. This led to a mushrooming of the number of things that were tracked: attendance, lateness, attitude, progress and many, many more were all analysed and discussed in meetings that could never have taken place before, with someone placed in charge of ensuring each of these numbers went the right way.

Proficiency with data came to be seen as a key part of being a competent teacher or leader and was woven formally into the *Teachers' Standards* (Department for Education, 2011). While ITT providers have been slow (perhaps deliberately and wisely) to incorporate this into their curriculums, they have been unable to protect their trainees from the numbers onslaught once they are employed in schools. Questioning the data is often heresy. Teachers expressing unease about data were seen to be making excuses for their own poor performance and most learned to keep quiet if they wanted their careers to advance. Those judged to be performing well by the spreadsheets sensibly kept their heads down and said nothing.

In many schools, data came to be regarded as a good in itself, and the more of it the better. It is for this reason that many schools now insist their teachers enter data six times a year, whereas at one time, an end-of-year grade was thought perfectly adequate.

This – an example of groupthink on a massive scale – has done enormous damage. The lack of thought or overall strategic planning and the gradual, somnolent way in which data capture and analysis has rolled through our schools has had all sorts of damaging unintended effects. The disaster is very well described by Ian Malcolm in *Jurassic Park* as he reacts with horror to the genetic wizardry that has led to the resurrection of the dinosaurs: 'Your scientists were so preoccupied with whether or not they could,' he says, 'that they didn't stop to think if they should.'

The first unintended consequence could easily have been avoided if some time had been taken to properly think things through. To get any meaningful information from a large volume of data, the data must be standardised. To be compared, numbers must mean the same thing. Schools that want to track and analyse data cannot use different assessment systems. For example, it is impossible for maths to use a 9–1 score and for a history department to use letters A–G if those in charge of analysing the data want to make comparisons. Most schools now insist that all subjects use one system, which is very often based on GCSE grades applied to every pupil from Year 7 to 11. This drive to standardise warps curriculum and assessment as all departments have to make children of all ages do GCSE-style questions in the tests used to grade them. Some, of course, choose not to; but these, whether wilfully or accidentally, are actually subverting the purpose of the overall system, which is to give those overseeing the data an understanding of how the school's pupils will perform at the end of Year 11. Many departments now teach directly to the tests, narrowing the curriculum and warping traditional academic disciplines into the often-crude mark schemes and rubrics used to assess them by exam boards.

Attempts to assess the accuracy of the numbers placed on school data systems and spreadsheets may actually be impossible. While agreeing on what constitutes one grade is easier in quantitative subjects such as maths and physics, in qualitative subjects like history and English it is much, much more difficult. This was acknowledged by Ofqual in 2018 when they revealed huge grade variations between different markers (Hymas, 2018).

If experienced exam markers can't agree on what grade pupils should be given on a final public examination, how realistic is it to expect teachers to do the same on internal tests? Any grade assigned to any child in these subjects – be it in their final formal exam or half-termly on an internal spreadsheet – is actually based on the how the person marking it interprets the mark scheme and it is very difficult even for very experienced teachers to get a meaningful and replicable shared understanding. This makes agonising over subtle variations at best a waste of time and at worst, when this results in knee-jerk reactions, poorly thought-through actions that may do actual harm. While proactive departments will try to minimise variation through moderation of work and training of less experienced teachers, the very best that can be achieved is a general consistency within the department, usually based on the views of the department head because those less senior will, whether consciously or subconsciously, revise their marking to match the interpretation of more senior colleagues.

Even if consistency is achieved within a department (which it often isn't), the agreed interpretation of the mark scheme is unlikely to be shared by a department of the same subject in a different school or the person who ends up marking final exams.

Confusing matters further, the inexact, uncertain nature of the process means that the subjective judgement made by teachers is likely to be affected by what they know – or indeed think they know – about individual pupils they interact with from day to day; prior attainment, behaviour, demographic and even handwriting may all feed into the grade teachers give (Henry, 2013). When grades are formative and used by teachers as a rule-of-thumb working measure, this problem isn't as severe because everyone understands that they aren't empirical. Unfortunately though, as soon as a grade goes onto a spreadsheet it assumes power disproportionate to its reliability. When this happens the mismatch between the power of the data and its utility becomes very concerning because it means any actions put in place in response may not be valid.

The drive for standardisation also ignores important differences between subjects and can result in ludicrous comparisons – for example, judging a BTEC assessed exclusively through coursework as doing better than a GCSE assessed through an examination simply because more pupils get a top grade, and then using this to make judgements about the quality of teaching in each department.

Given the power that data and the spreadsheets used to examine it have in schools, the validity of the numbers with which they are populated deserves more attention than it usually gets. Perhaps the reason this isn't looked into too closely is because even a cursory examination reveals significant problems, and there are now just too many vested interests for there to be real appetite to work through, understand and respond to the profound implications.

Firstly, almost all the data used in secondary schools comes from the results of two tests, in English and maths, that children sit at the end of their primary education. A target for every child in every subject is set from an average of these two scores. This means that a child's eventual target grade in subjects as diverse as geography, music, drama, German, art and PE is formed on the basis of how they did in tests in completely different subjects. To make matters even worse, there are big question marks over the validity of the data generated from these tests, which are examined in a way that allows schools to cheat or manipulate scores if they wish to (Kingsnorth, 2018).

The data on the spreadsheets simply isn't robust enough to be as used as it is and this raises some uncomfortable ethical questions; if the data isn't valid in the first place then the actions that schools take in response to this data will not be valid either. For example, the setting of children, which has an enormous impact on teacher expectation and the work children do, may not actually be based on reliable information, making any impact profoundly troubling. This may generate even more spreadsheet-based work for teachers who have to justify why a child or group isn't at a level that may actually be entirely unrealistic.

Even if the data that went into the spreadsheets were watertight, the way in which it is used is often amateurish. To be blunt, many of those in charge of data in schools lack the statistical literacy to do their jobs properly. For example, many schools seem to have real trouble understanding that correlation is not the same thing as causation – which, for example, is why posters equating drops in attendance to a proportional drop in an eventual GCSE grade can be found in the corridors of schools all over the country. What has been misunderstood here is quite clear: while being in school or not may well have an effect on exam results, the reasons behind a pupil's poor or good attendance are probably just as important. These subtle, powerful factors – maybe a background of poor health or parents who don't think school that important and so take their children out for cheaper term-time holidays – are the main reason for disappointing exam results, with the actual attendance figure just a symptom of a more important underlying problem, or indeed combination of problems. The general misunderstanding around correlation and causation is memorably illustrated by an old story, perhaps apocryphal, about U2's Bono trying to illustrate the scale of the AIDS epidemic in Africa by saying at a concert, 'Every time I click my fingers, someone dies' – to which a member of the audience shouts back 'Then just stop doing it!'

Over-emphasising the importance of what can be easily measured at the expense of what cannot is a well-known issue both in and beyond education, and is often termed the McNamara fallacy after the American secretary of defence between 1961 and 1968 in charge of the Vietnam War. McNamara believed that success or failure could be measured by counting bodies: if one side was killing more than the other, it was winning. This just wasn't true. Greater numbers of Viet Cong fighters meant that they could sustain greater losses than the American public would tolerate of its own army. McNamara's fixation on something that could be easily measured meant neglecting the wider factors; although they consistently out-killed the North Vietnamese, they lost the war. Addiction to certain numbers and the subsequent neglect of harder-to-measure factors is having a detrimental effect on England's children for similar reasons. Instead of being seen as an indicative measure, the numbers going into the spreadsheets have come to be seen as goals in themselves, masking the more subtle and difficult-to-measure wider issues that are likely to be much more significant.

School leadership should not be held solely responsible for this misapplication. School accountability agencies (the DfE and Ofsted so often the tail that wags the dog) have in the past used data just as stupidly. Mistakes made over how to fairly hold schools and teachers accountable for pupils' results has meant that fluctuations in the numbers on spreadsheets have often been assumed to be far more significant than is actually the case, especially given that very extensive recent change in examination formats means that like is rarely compared to like. Few schools apply basic statistical principles such as sample size, averages, standard deviation, statistical significance or an understanding of the difference between aggregated and disaggregated data to the numbers. The failure to do this means that any trends or patterns, however apparently clear, may not actually be particularly revealing, making actions undertaken as a result of them invalid. While Ofsted does have specialist data analysis teams there is no requirement for teams to call these in and it is likely that some inspectors lack the statistical understanding to know whether they should or not, which means there isn't much incentive for schools to apply these statistical safeguards either, given that these may not be taken into account by those whose judgement matters most. Finally, it is also worth considering the possibility that data literacy in schools just isn't high enough for those that run them to know when they should challenge an inspectorate's interpretation of their figures.

Statistical illiteracy at all levels has created even more spreadsheet-based work because it has resulted in schools expecting their teachers to analyse data that may well be completely invalid. In some schools teachers are expected to work on class-level data in a process usually called gap analysis, even though the small sample sizes involved make any findings of no use whatsoever. For example, a teacher may be asked to analyse the performance of different subgroups within their exam class to find out where their extra intervention work should take place. This may seem sensible, but if the group contains only two pupil premium pupils and these are underperforming, it is not necessarily appropriate to make changes in response because there just aren't enough of them to know whether this underperformance is to do with their demographic group or a result of individual issues or personal characteristics.

More problems can be seen in the creation of demographic groups made up of pupils with supposed similarities. In schools this is common, with spreadsheets used to assess how well these groups are doing compared to other groups and the cohort as a whole. The problem here is that this data, often referred to as disaggregated data because it breaks overall figures into smaller components, is actually also aggregated because those in each group may actually have very little in common with each other and is itself comprised of children of very diverse backgrounds – just because two pupils eat free school meals does not mean the issues affecting their educational attainment will be the same. An understanding of this and a search for more nuance has led some schools to break down groups into smaller and smaller subgroups, creating such categories as 'white boys on free school meals' or 'black pupil premium girls', which creates more and more spreadsheet-based tasks, which are usually pointless because the smaller these groups, the less likely any pattern found is to be at all statistically significant. For some teachers and leaders this sort of work can be very addictive, with a lot of time wasted sifting through numbers in the search for something revealing. Such searches are usually quixotic; in reality the process is often as pointless as picking up a handful of pebbles from a beach, noting their colour and then using this information to make predictions about the overall colour of an entirely different stretch of sand a hundred miles down the coast.

Schools are fertile ground for this sort of thing because data-led accountability measures and targetism created contexts in which heavy intervention on selected small groups of pupils was seen as more desirable than focusing on making general improvements that were beneficial to all. If one group of pupils are, or seem to be, performing at a lower level than their classmates, it looks logical to give this group extra help because if their results improve, so the thinking goes, those of the cohort as a whole will too. This has caused schools and the teachers who work in them to use their spreadsheets to find these underperforming groups, whether or not the sample size is large enough to make any trends significant or whether those in the group actually have very much in common with each other. Even if these groups were statistically significant and homogeneous – which are often mutually exclusive – there remain ethical issues around treating a child differently because of their background. It is even possible damage is done by labelling pupils as something they aren't or making them think they have special requirements they do not really have, or are deserving of particular help just because of who they happen to be. This does not necessarily mean that grouping pupils is always wrong, but the consequences, beneficial and not so, should be thought through very carefully.

Regrettably, not many schools have paused at all. Far more common has been a headlong rush to a full acceptance of the primacy of the numbers with those questioning the figures seen as outcasts in many schools. In response, data-management companies have made the claim that they have the ability to make sense of the cacophony of data. All this creates even more spreadsheet-based work for teachers because such programmes need a regular stream of data to feed on, making entering this an increasingly time-consuming part of a teacher's role.

In summary, the reason there are so many spreadsheets is that new technology provides the means to capture more data than ever before and those managing it often do not have the knowledge or skills to do so properly. Even those who do have the necessary expertise often find themselves powerless because the inspectorates that exist to hold schools to account also use data crudely, making a nuanced understanding of no advantage. The unquestioning acceptance of data and its analysis has created an entire industry around the numbers, with companies producing and maintaining systems designed to manage data sustaining themselves by selling improvements, which often mean the ability to capture an ever-larger volume. These companies have no interest in the validity of the numbers they crunch. This, coupled with the belief that more data is always better than less data, has increased both the frequency and intensity of analysis for many teachers. In the fetishization of numbers, what they represent has been forgotten, throwing disciplines completely out of kilter and obscuring the point of education altogether. Finally, data-analysis companies have been quick to take advantage of statistical ignorance in schools by pushing progression models that appear sensible but are actually almost entirely spurious because the numbers they run on are not valid. The result has been catastrophic. Thousands of teachers in English schools are wasting working hours and taxpayer money poring over numbers, figures, graphs and charts that show nothing of any meaning, thereby being robbed of time they could spend on improving their teaching, assessing intelligently or developing inspiring curriculums.

Jurassic Park's Dr Malcolm was indeed right. We became so preoccupied with whether we could, we didn't think hard enough about whether we should – and the effects have been devastating.

What to do

Hearteningly, Ofsted's latest framework does meaningfully respond to many of these issues. In the future, inspection teams have been instructed not to look at internal progress data at all. This could well be a powerful stimulus for change, but only if schools respond intelligently and imaginatively to this opportunity. Worryingly, the form isn't good; when national curriculum levels were abolished, many (if not all) schools responded by simply shoving GCSE tracking down to all years, replicating exactly the same problems. It is likely that even if Ofsted's new framework does begin driving changes in schools there will be an inevitable lag before many schools begin fighting their addiction to data.

In the meantime the teachers in them will need to continue working with or around the numbers.

This is tough. A thread running through a lot of the work of Mark Enser (@ EnserMark on Twitter) – a geography teacher and head of department – is that left alone to their own devices most teachers will gradually move towards effective teaching. There is a compelling logic to this. All teachers want their pupils to learn quickly and few are dogmatic enough to stick to methods for purely ideological reasons when they prove not to work in practice. The reason this doesn't happen as much as it should is interfering external factors that remove autonomy, like prescriptive teaching and learning policies which force teachers to do things against their better judgement.

Few teachers, given a choice, would spend much time on spreadsheets when they could be doing more meaningful things – or indeed not working at all. Teachers spend time analysing data because they are told to, not because they think it is useful to their work. If they had a choice, they wouldn't, which makes finding ways to reduce or even eliminate it very tricky.

It is important to acknowledge the professional constraints under which we must operate. Most institutions, in education or not, pursue policies that some of their employees disagree with, and these cannot be ignored even when they are just plain wrong. Working as team means holding the line even when we disagree. However tempting it is to do so, we cannot refuse to follow official direction because by doing so we undermine the entire institution, including its positive aspects. Furthermore, refusing to do or ignoring a directed task – whether that's analysing nonsensical data or anything else – undermines our credibility, positions us as troublemakers and so makes sound reasoning and logic easier to ignore. However frustrating it is, teachers working in schools that require them to complete extensive spreadsheet work should do it as well as they can, or leave their schools for environments in which it is not required.

This said, there is nothing unprofessional about spending as little time as possible on work that has no impact – or even a negative one – on pupils. If a school demands data is entered but does not require that individual teachers analyse it then they should not. If schools demand that the data is analysed pointlessly, teachers should do the minimum expected of them and should avoid being sucked into doing more just because some of their colleagues do or because this impresses SLTs. To work out what is meaningful and what is not, it is a good idea to spend some time becoming statistically literate and learning how sample size, significance, standard deviation and the difference between aggregated and disaggregated data affects the validity of the figures. Teachers who do this are likely to also find themselves in a better position to respectfully and positively challenge flawed policies and procedures. And they should. Teachers who do challenge bad policy are behaving both professionally and ethically because by doing so they are representing the interests of their pupils.

Challenging those in charge of data is not easy. These people – usually high in the food chain, be they members of SLT or data management professionals – have a vested interest in the status quo because accepting that their methods are flawed means accepting that their own roles are far less meaningful than they had thought, and that they may even be doing more harm than good. This is tough for anyone to swallow and particularly so for good people who genuinely believe they are doing a good job. To make matters worse, there is often little appetite at a school's highest levels for opening a discussion around the spreadsheets because the years in which the numbers have been sacrosanct have created an environment in which many school leaders, including many heads, honestly no longer know how to run a school without them. Removing the comfort blanket must feel terrifying to those who have convinced themselves that the numbers are accurate, meaningful and a fair measure of how the school is doing because it exposes them as knowing much, much less than they thought they did.

All this means real and lasting change is likely to be more a product of evolution than it is revolution in most contexts.

Teachers who've gained a reasonable understanding of how data does and does not work in a school and who want to begin the process of trying to effect change might start by pretending they know less than they actually do. Phrasing concerns as questions (and then backing off) gives those with influence the time and space to do some thinking of their own and allows them at least the chance to make adjustments while keeping face. Saying 'Hey! You know, that data we're analysing isn't statistically significant. Why do you make us do it?' is far less likely to have an impact than saying 'Um, I've been doing some reading and I don't really understand how statistical significance works. Can you explain it to me using the data from one of my classes? It looks to me as if the way I'm doing things isn't meaningful, although I'm sure it's just something I haven't understood.'

Teachers asked to complete 'gap analysis' on groups too small to be statistically significant can illustrate the flaw in such processes by using spurious differences to point out the potential for distraction this sort of activity can provide. This could mean analysing the difference in performance between those who are left- or right-handed, those who live in odd- or even-numbered houses or blondes or non-blondes to show how inappropriate number crunching can raise false flags and place emphasis on the wrong areas. Of course, teachers doing this should ensure this is also done sensitively and privately and steer clear away from any approach that might embarrass the person they are trying to convince to change. As always, it is helpful to bear in mind the charity principle – accepting that people who have applied or even developed flawed policies of any type have usually done so with good intentions and have made rational choices based on the information available.

Teachers at any position in the hierarchy who want to bring about change, whether this is to do with data or indeed anything else, might also be wise to remember it is easier to shift when a sensible, thoughtful alternative is offered. This will inevitably look different across disciplines and contexts and so any generic advice will probably not be helpful.

Doing all this does not guarantee success. There may be no appetite at all for change given the enormous implications and the transformation in how a school might have to operate. Teachers who find themselves ignored and dismissed even after polite and thoughtful attempts to initiate change are left with a stark choice (as those reading this book sequentially will notice is becoming a bit of a theme): either go along with the madness because it is compensated for by the positive aspects of the institutions for which they work – or leave.

Both of these, in different circumstances, are rational choices.

Teachers who do choose to leave because of their school's poor data use should, where possible and without rancour, be clear that this is the reason they have looked for and secured employment elsewhere. Too much in teaching is left unsaid, which is a significant reason for the multitude of valueless activities that go on in schools.

If schools realise they lose good staff when they refuse to act upon legitimate, professional concerns they may – eventually – get the message.

Why is everyone so scared of Ofsted?

High noon at Gasworks High and someone on the administrative team gets The Call. The message goes straight to the head, who tells their deputy and then the rest of the senior leadership team. Everything, clubs, revision sessions, staff training and all meetings are cancelled; and, after school, the whole quivering staff is called together. The party line is read out and the school's non-negotiables reiterated.

Finally the assembled teachers are told to get some rest.

Assuming this is a joke, everyone laughs, which, after a moment of confusion, the head finds secretly very reassuring.

By then The Call will have rippled out of the building. Childcare will be rearranged. All evening plans – from a midweek trip to the pub to a meal booked a year ago to celebrate a wedding anniversary – will be cancelled. On the way home, after leaving school late in the evening, teachers will stop to stock up on energy drinks, instant noodles and sugary snacks. Former smokers will relapse. At home, lamp-lit and ashen-faced, teachers will sit at their desks and plan, make resources, mark, populate data sheets, and then re-plan. In the early hours they will sneak into bed beside worried partners who don't know what to say or do to help.

There, they'll lie awake, hoping that their classes will behave and praying an inspector will not come in period 4 to see 9Y5.

And that if they do, please God make sure Josh isn't in.

And then, in many schools, the same thing will happen the following day too. At the end of the second day they will wait in the staffroom until the head, crying tears of either joy or despair, emerges from that final meeting.

What they say will, for better or worse, mark out the beat to which the school will dance for the coming years.

Drop any false bravado and be honest.

Most teachers are scared of Ofsted and some are terrified. We have been for such a long time that the fear has become sort of accepted as inevitable. A sort of fairy-tale troll, Ofsted and its inspectors are talked about in the same hushed tones as Ringwraiths in *Lord of the Rings*. It has a degree of wide cultural penetration achieved by the inspectorate of no other industry. Stand-up comedians make jokes about it without the need to explain.

Fear of Ofsted has become so accepted, it is easy to feel as if the organisation has been designed to be scary.

But nobody wants things this way. Teachers most certainly do not. Nor do school leaders. Despite how it might seem in the midst of the process, inspectors are not monsters and (with perhaps the odd sadistic exception) do not take pleasure in inflicting fear and misery. Ofsted has always said it wants to see normal operation, and a school staffed by sleep-deprived, crazed zombies doing things they don't usually do serves nobody's interests. Amanda Spielman, England's Chief Inspector of Schools, clarified this recently, saying, 'Ofsted inspections should not be a performance that schools spend hours rehearsing' (Vaughan, 2017). While any assurance that schools should just operate in exactly the way they always do is probably a bit fanciful given just how much is at stake, there is no reason to believe these assurances are not genuine.

So if nobody wants us so scared, why are we?

First, it is important to be clear that not *all* of us are, and the degree of fear varies.

In schools where results are good, Ofsted is less frightening than it is for those working in places where outcomes are poor, because those in the former group can be more confident of a favourable judgement. Since 2010, when the contextual value added (CVA) measurement was removed, accountability frameworks have effectively assumed that exam outcomes are the product of a school's work alone, which means any school where progress is below the national average, regardless of any contextual difficulties it faces, feels more threatened than those with above-average results (Nye and Rollett, 2017). It is also important to note that 'outstanding' schools remain exempt from inspection, which means those who work in these will experience much less fear than schools sitting on lower grades.

Teachers are scared of Ofsted, not so much because of the process of inspection itself, but because they are afraid of a negative outcome. It is the judgements of 'requires improvement' and 'inadequate' that are actually the real sources of fear.

To understand why, let's begin by considering what happens to a school's management after an 'inadequate' judgement.

First, even if the school chooses to appeal against aspects of the report (a process that very rarely results in any significant change and relies on an in-depth knowledge of the Ofsted handbook), the headteacher is quite likely to lose their job. Headteachers that have been in post for five years or more only have around a 20% chance of keeping their job three years after an 'inadequate' judgement. For those in position between two and four years, only around 40% will still be the head three years after the bad report. Those appointed less than two years before the inspection generally fare much better (probably because they can better make the case that the school's failings aren't their fault), with 80% still in place three years after inspection – which somewhat skews the overall figure of around a quarter moving on within three years (Lynch et al., 2017).

While most of those who leave choose to resign to avoid the indignity of the sack, the professional effect often amounts to the same thing. The report will be reported in local media in hyperbolic and often hysterical terms. Even when the immediate hoo-ha dies down, the report will be available on the Ofsted website in perpetuity. Colleagues, family and friends will all get to know about what amounts to a distinctly public disgrace.

Many heads in this position are facing the end of their leadership career and some will never step into a school again.

However professionally deserved a bad judgement, it would be heartless to have no personal sympathy. Headteachers, by and large and like most of us, entered teaching because they wanted to do something morally purposeful with their lives and do their best. The shame of an 'inadequate' judgement, deserved or not, can be devastating to self-esteem and a particularly brutal, unkind end to a typically long career spent in public service. An assistant headteacher working in a school judged as 'inadequate' in 2012, who wishes to remain anonymous (it is revealing just how often anonymity was insisted upon by teachers I spoke with about this chapter), told me that immediately after the feedback the head 'cleared her desk and that was the last we saw of her'. And while he actually agreed with the judgement, he went on to say that the process 'ended the careers of some talented teachers and caused all staff (hardworking and dedicated staff) a great deal of stress and worry. A lot of personal and professional friends of mine either left the school or the profession and I will always regret this was, and is still, allowed to happen to good and dedicated people.'

Ofsted, of course, will claim this is not their fault. Recently, Sean Harford, on Twitter, said 'I think it's the current knee jerk reaction and lack of intelligent use of inspection information that's the problem: more support needed, less "moving on" of leaders and others by those who make decisions based on inspection outcomes.' He may well be right, but this will be cold comfort to those whose professional – and sometimes personal – lives have been destroyed by a culture that Ofsted says is nothing to do with them. Some won't accept this at all and will say that this is just another example of the buck being pushed around. Those with this perspective might draw on the stark brutality of the term 'inadequate' and may suggest that this in itself leaves governing bodies and other decision makers feeling they have no other option but to remove those identified as such. This, of course, is even more understandable in a context in which such decision making has become normalised; it's always more comforting to be in the herd than it is to stand alone. It is actually probably fair to go beyond this. Given the devastating effects on a school's reputation and the performative effect that a bad Ofsted report has on this, it is quite logical for governors to want to make it clear that they are acting decisively in order to limit the damage. Removing leadership sends out a strong signal – especially given that their own competence is also likely to be questioned in the report.

Deputies and members of the leadership team, unless recently appointed or lucky enough to be individually named positively in the report, may not last much longer. Any school deemed to be 'inadequate' overall is very likely to get the same rating for leadership and management and almost certainly will not get a rating above 'requires improvement' in this category. This judgement percolates down from the head to leaders at all levels. One assistant headteacher at a school judged 'inadequate' who chose to stay in position described the year after the report as 'undoubtedly the worst year of my teaching career, constantly worried about the future'.

Even department heads, particularly those leading areas identified as underperforming in the report, may feel vulnerable. Those that do choose to stay will know that they are likely to face great pressure and change when new senior leadership takes over and that short-term survival in no way guarantees long-term security. If leadership is judged not to have the capacity to make the improvements demanded by the report, the school will go into special measures, bringing even more serious consequences and typically resulting in dramatic changes to day-to-day life in the school. Any category 4 judgement means almost inevitable academisation for schools still under LEA jurisdiction, which, again, is likely to mean significant and far-reaching change, exhausting for those who remain whether it's positive or negative.

The consequences of a 'requires improvement' judgement, while not as immediately dramatic, can still be extremely unpleasant. Such schools often face a monitoring visit the following year and another full inspection the year after that. In the meantime the leadership of schools in this position, working under a perpetual sword of Damocles, will be forced to take support, whether wanted or not, from outside the school, which removes autonomy and can be acutely professionally embarrassing. Heads and senior leaders will be expected to at least appear to be accepting it, which may actually do more harm than good because this support is often provided by leaders working in very different contexts who don't have an adequate understanding of the issues faced by schools they are supposed to be helping. Indeed, those who may actually be most able to help may be precluded from doing so because they are more likely to be working in schools given one of the two lowest grades by Ofsted. This issue was raised by the Education Policy Institute in 2016, when they concluded the 'Key findings' section of their accountability, assessment and inspection report by writing:

> If Ofsted judgements are too harsh for many high performing schools with high disadvantage/low prior attainment, then this may be deterring good teachers and leaders from taking on such schools, and will mean that the DFE is less able to use the leaders in these schools for 'system leadership', since this is often linked to the Ofsted grade. (Hutchinson, 2016)

This, I hope, explains why heads and senior leadership teams are right to fear negative Ofsted judgements.

Less immediately clear is why this fear is also felt by rank-and-file staff, who are not specifically identified on the report and far less likely to be shamed and then removed from their positions.

The most obvious reason is similar to the fears of SLT. Working in a category 4 school can feel humiliating, especially for those who care most about doing a good job and being well regarded professionally. Such a damning label – referred to as 'a mark of Cain' by one teacher I spoke with – can be a paralysing body blow. This is not at all irrational. Schools can indeed be wary about recruiting or even interviewing teachers who have come from an 'inadequate' school. Even the most confident and able practitioners may doubt themselves and begin second guessing what they do. Another teacher told me they stopped taking part in TeachMeets and conferences because they felt their contributions had been undermined by their 'inadequate' Ofsted label, which as well as being really sad also suggests that such a judgement may have a negative impact on staff development, making it harder for the school to improve.

However it is spun, telling anyone you work at an 'inadequate' school can easily make you feel inadequate and feelings of inadequacy are paralysing.

Even teachers who do not tie their identity up in their school's Ofsted rating may find it very difficult to escape the shadow cast by the anxiety of their colleagues. Heads and SLT are only human and, consciously or unconsciously, often pass their own fear down to others; and badly rated schools – or those feeling threatened by the perceived likelihood of a bad rating – can become permeated by a sense of dread. This may be explicitly articulated; but even when it is not, the effects for ordinary teachers can be significant: fear causes stress, which frays tempers, which contributes to irrational decision making, bullying and hardheartedness. While it is comforting to believe that adversity invariably binds people together, this is often not true. Frequently, great pressure is just as likely – perhaps actually more likely – to incentivise 'every man for themselves' self-preservation at the expense of what is best for the community as a whole.

Anxieties are worsened by the way in which Ofsted inspections are organised and run. Because Ofsted is only in schools for a comparatively short period of time, what they observe becomes enormously high-stakes because it is taken to be representative of the way in which the school typically functions.

Of course this isn't logical. Teachers are more effective with some classes than they are with others; and although of course it shouldn't, behaviour can also vary wildly within a school. If a teacher is lucky and an inspector happens to see a lesson in which children behave and work well, this may be used as evidence that children in the school work well generally. If, instead, an inspector comes to a lesson in which children behave badly and learn nothing, this might form part of an evidence base that this is typical. It is this uncertainty which probably keeps teachers awake at night before inspections more than anything else. It is also important to note that the unreliability of lesson observation as a method of assessing teaching quality is now fairly well accepted. While Ofsted claims that it understands this and doesn't grade lessons, it remains unclear, at least among teachers, how Ofsted can come to an overall teaching rating for a school if it doesn't somehow aggregate ratings of the lessons its inspectors see. Even if Ofsted is right and their methodology is sound, the message is not getting through and the lack of clarity around this contributes to the very high pressure that teachers feel when an inspector enters their classroom.

So it is little wonder that inspection feels so utterly terrifying. Teachers who know their school has poor results and is in danger of falling into 'requires improvement' – or, worse, 'inadequate' – regard themselves as being under enormous pressure to perform well on inspection days. They may be right or wrong to feel this pressure, but the anxiety is the same.

Whether management remains in place or not, a school placed in the bottom two Ofsted categories will face significant change. An 'inadequate' rating (and a 'requires improvement' to a lesser extent) is a clear judgement that what the school is doing is not working and that urgent change is required. Senior leaders – whether they are justified in doing so or just want to appear decisive to protect their leadership rating – may feel pressure to make wholesale alterations to structures, staffing, curriculum and policy. In order to ensure that these changes are being properly implemented, there is also likely to be a proportionate increase in monitoring, which increases workload and can feel oppressive.

These changes – necessary or otherwise – make a school a more stressful place in which to work. One of the ways humans cope with complexity (and schools are enormously complex) is by learning processes and then automating them, freeing up brain space to think about other things. Sudden, dramatic changes make automated processes redundant and mean that tasks have to be relearned. This is exhausting and, on top of inevitably increased workloads and the emotional impact of the poor judgement, can quickly make a school feel like an unbearable place in which to be. Schools can be very quickly utterly transformed and teachers who are able to do so may feel this is a good time to move on (especially those who know they are effective and resent having to constantly evidence this), which reinforces this sense of unfamiliarity for remaining staff and may create a vicious circle. Those that do stay may only do so because they cannot secure new roles, either because they genuinely aren't competent or because of the stigma of coming from a school publicly announced to be failing.

Of course, a failing school needs to be identified so it can be turned around; and if all, or even most, schools getting 'inadequate' ratings or being put into special measures quickly improved and obtained good or better judgements, teachers might be less afraid of working in one. Unfortunately, the picture is much patchier than this. Writing in 2013, Loic Menzies found that less than half of schools rated in the bottom two Ofsted categories achieved an improved rating (Menzies, 2013).

For some schools, a bad Ofsted judgement kicks them down so hard that it takes them years to get up again, and a few never do. These are closed down, merged with other schools or academised – which, in a process some might see as a rather clever but dishonest sleight of hand, leads to their old Ofsted ratings being effectively expunged (Robertson, 2017). Some schools that do survive may bounce between academy chains and suffer near-annual wholesale changes to leadership, which may result in new policy and restructuring every year.

One teacher working at such a school in the Midlands tells of a newly appointed head beginning their first assembly by saying earnestly, 'My commitment to you is I will stay the whole of this year' – as if this was something worth shouting about. (In actual fact, they did not even manage that.) Schools finding themselves in this position enter a vicious circle from which it requires herculean effort to break free.

Such schools, very often in areas where it is already difficult to find and keep good teachers, may find themselves haemorrhaging staff. Often forbidden from hiring trainees or NQTs by the conditions of the report (Department for Education, 2018), schools in this position may feel compelled to appoint applicants they would not normally consider, and experienced, effective teachers are far less likely to look beyond the latest report. Research for the Institute for Education by Sam Sims found further worrying implications of this on the English education system as a whole. In the conclusion of his paper 'High-stakes accountability and teacher turnover', Sims wrote that 'one third of the teachers that leave schools regraded "inadequate" move on to teach in other schools and a third of these "movers" find jobs in relatively ineffective schools, where they are less likely to improve their teaching. A group of ineffective teachers may therefore be churning round the English school system' (Sims, 2016).

Ofsted, quite understandably, argues that reports must be publicly available in order for parents to understand the quality of education their children are receiving. However, we need to be clear and honest about the performative nature of the inspection process and that publishing results can cause further issues for already floundering schools. No parent is happy with their child attending a bad school and this means those with the wherewithal to be aware and act upon the publicly available information are likely to fight to keep their child out of a school with a bad rating.

Parents who can afford to do so will even take the Ofsted ratings of local schools into account when choosing where to live, with the Ofsted ratings of nearby schools, if they are good, published by estate agents as a matter of course. This information is powerful enough to drive up house prices in the area and so alter demographics. This means that those children who do attend 'inadequate' schools are more likely to be those with parents who (for whatever reason) lack the ability to secure their child a place elsewhere. Such children are, to be blunt, frequently harder to teach than the national average. 'Inadequate' schools are also far more likely to be undersubscribed and these free spaces are often filled by children with atypical educational experiences. A teacher working in a school given an 'inadequate' judgement told me that the Year 7 pupil intake went from 210 the year before the inspection to only 130 the year after it, which led to a reduction in funding and redundancies, lowering morale and making it even harder for the school to improve.

A bad Ofsted judgement is also likely to have serious implications on pupil morale and motivation. The announcement of an 'inadequate' judgement is likely to demoralise conscientious pupils while providing others with an excuse to stop working hard or even behaving. If your school is a terrible one, then what is the point of doing what your teachers tell you to do?

The high-stakes, high-profile nature of inspection makes schools competitive and pits schools against each other. Ofsted ratings are a zero-sum game. 'Outstanding' only has value as a judgement if other schools are judged to be less effective. Schools who achieve the highest ratings plaster them all over signage and stationery, causing house prices to rise and attracting more children from traditionally academic, aspirational backgrounds. Schools with poor Ofsted ratings suffer the reverse and the longer a school retains a poor judgement, the harder it may become for it to make the changes required to improve its rating. Sadly, in some cases, the first judgement intended to spark necessary improvement may actually be a contributory cause of further decline. Ofsted will, of course, say that this isn't their problem; they are just highlighting issues and it is up to the school to improve. They will point to the fact that some schools do improve as evidence that what they do works. My contention is that this is at least somewhat disingenuous because in some circumstances Ofsted makes improvement harder, and that it is irresponsible to undermine an already struggling school if this is likely to make it harder for it to get better.

Ofsted is most helpful to those who need it the least, and least helpful to those who need help the most.

Given the dizzyingly high stakes of inspections in England, those who work in schools are quite right to be very afraid of a negative outcome.

All this said, it would be unfair not to discuss the recent changes Ofsted has made to itself. Wisely, Amanda Spielman, the Chief Inspector of Schools in England, has tried to address the shortcomings of the input-output model in Ofsted's latest inspection framework. The new model, if fully implemented, puts less emphasis on examination results and more on curriculum, dividing this into intent, implementation and impact. More attention will be paid to what it calls 'quality of education', which on the face of it seems fairer as this means poor results should not necessarily doom a school to failure if it can demonstrate teaching is based on a coherent curriculum and delivered effectively. Although this does not mean outcomes will be ignored (Ofsted still maintains that strong intent and implementation should lead to strong results), it does mean that schools working in contexts where it is hard to achieve great results should, in theory at least, feel more confident that what they do to try to improve will be factored into final judgements. Ofsted has also promised to be more vigilant about ethically dubious practices designed only to improve published outcomes – be this narrowing curriculum, off-rolling pupils or entering them for qualifications that have little value to the child.

While this may (or may not) lead to better education overall, it seems unlikely these changes will in themselves reduce fear of Ofsted. Indeed it may actually increase overall anxiety as schools in areas where outcomes are traditionally strong may feel less confident that these can act as a sort of 'get out of jail free card', or a mask over poor practice once compensated for by tutoring, parental involvement or other factors.

It also appears as if this shift may actually simply be creating new sources of fear. It is not at all clear to many school leaders what Ofsted means by 'strong curriculum intent' and this may already be increasing workload, as schools begin frantic audits of schemes of work to try to make sure what they do will be deemed satisfactory by England's all-powerful accountability machine. This anxiety is very likely to drip onto teachers of all stripes, who may find themselves not only worrying about the results of their pupils but also fearing that even if these are good, they may still be found wanting.

Whatever and however Ofsted inspects, there will always be fear so long as the stakes remain as high as they are, and there appears to be no appetite to seriously reconsider a model that pits school against school.

Teachers simply cannot rely on Ofsted itself to become less scary.

The reason Ofsted makes us all anxious is that it has the capacity to inflict real damage for reasons often outside the control of individual teachers and because of unpredictability inherent to the way inspection is run.

Ofsted is frightening because a negative judgement may actually make it more difficult for a school to make the improvements it needs to.

Teachers and leaders in many schools are afraid of Ofsted because it is frightening.

What to do

Few credible people argue that we should not have an inspectorate at all. Schools run on taxpayer money and the public has the right to know how well this is being spent. But we need an inspectorate that is as kind and human as it is rigorous, and as tough as it is to strike this balance, we must. At a time in which we are finding it harder than ever to hire and keep teachers it is neither desirable nor even necessary for teachers to live in fear. Those who work in schools are not ruthless, high-rolling, risk-taking piratical business executives and nor are they candidates on *The Apprentice*. Education is, or at least should be, a moral profession and there should be no place for blood on the carpet, childish machismo or professional humiliation.

Lucy Crehan's *Cleverlands* shows England's school accountability system to be unusually myopic, and that most of the world's highest performing systems take a more nuanced and sophisticated approach to school underperformance. At the heart of this is an understanding that when things go wrong it is usually because of lots of different contextual factors and not just the incompetence of teachers and leaders. This allows for multifaceted, multi-agency support which deals with all the problems and avoids wasting time in confrontational finger-pointing. We need an inspectorate that sees things in the round because not doing so means ignoring important causes of underachievement. Crehan thinks the most effective system at dealing with underperformance is Shanghai's, which recognises the role played by context in that it uses effective leaders from schools working with similar challenges to lead change in underperforming schools – which is of course entirely logical once we accept, as we should, that a school's circumstances affect its operation (Worth et al., 2017; Lynch et al., 2017).

We have allowed Ofsted to evolve into such a blunt instrument because for too long we laboured under the fallacy that there is a perfect correlation between school input and pupil results. This caused us to ignore everything else that had an impact and led to the shouting down of those who raised concerns with a cry of 'low expectations'. This is so confused and poorly thought-through that, bizarrely, Ofsted reports may even acknowledge a school's unique challenges – for example, noting that it has a very high percentage of children who start and leave at non-standard times – but then completely ignoring this information when making their final judgement.

Regrettably, there is nothing most individual teachers working in schools can do to change the nature of inspection frameworks. But even working within the flawed system, there are strategies that can help.

The surest – and most depressingly reductive – is only to work in schools likely to get good Ofsted ratings, which will most often mean working and living in London, or comparatively affluent areas. The figures are pretty clear. While there are exceptions, by and large the more disadvantaged the demographic a school serves, the more likely it is to be rated either 'inadequate' or 'requires improvement'. Schools in more advantaged areas are far more likely to be rated 'good' or 'outstanding'. The Education Policy Institute's accountability, assessment and inspection report, published in 2016, finds that:

> Secondary schools with up to 5 per cent of pupils eligible for free school meals (FSM) are over three times as likely to be rated 'outstanding' as schools with at least 23 per cent FSM (48 per cent compared with 14 per cent 'outstanding'). Those secondary schools with the most FSM pupils are much more likely to be rated 'inadequate' than those with the fewest (15 per cent compared with 1 per cent). (Hutchinson, 2016)

These findings can be interpreted one of two ways. Either teachers and leaders tend to be weaker in poorer areas, or leading and teaching in richer areas tends to be easier. Whatever you believe (and I'll leave you to make up your own mind), it doesn't change the fact that, most simply, if you want to reduce fear of Ofsted in the most certain way, your best bet is to find work in an all-girls, selective, positive Progress 8 score school in a posher area.

How depressing. Choosing schools on the basis of their likely Ofsted rating, while perhaps practical for individual teachers, is not a satisfactory solution, because good teachers avoiding schools and areas in which need is most acute perpetuates inequality. As irritating and damaging as the 'hero' teacher cliché is – and without for a moment suggesting that teachers should martyr themselves in quixotic tilts against structural inequality – it is my belief that most state-school teachers did not choose their career because they wanted as easy a life as possible educating only society's most privileged children.

The final part of this chapter is for those teachers who, for whatever reason, know they work in schools more at risk of negative Ofsted judgements and want practical suggestions on how to manage the anxiety of inspection.

Firstly, just knowing the truth helps. Three years ago, my last GCSE history group got approximately the same exam grades as my first as an NQT. If we do not take context into account, it would appear that my teaching was no better than it was almost 15 years ago. But of course it is, and knowing that the outcome of my work will vary depending (at least to some extent) on the context in which I teach means I need not become disillusioned when the results of my pupils do not go up each year. The same is true of knowing that it is harder for some schools to get good Ofsted ratings than it is for others; if we know this, we should be able to take judgements less personally and can immunise ourselves against the kind of self-flagellation and despondency that pushes teachers out of our profession. Understanding that inspection is limited means that we understand that judgements are often limited too, which can help us look apparent disaster in the eye without breaking down. It is unfair to say that acknowledging context has an impact on pupil outcomes means 'low expectations' and we should stop.

We are all quite capable of understanding that some circumstances make it harder for certain pupils to achieve without arriving at the position they are doomed to failure whatever we do. It is frustrating and insulting to be told that some schools achieving incredible results in challenging circumstances means that any concerns we have about the contexts in which ours operate are invalid. We get that it is possible for all schools to get better. We also get that it is harder for some of us than others. Most of us care very deeply and are constantly trying to improve – not because we are scared of Ofsted but because we care about doing our jobs well and want our pupils to have rich, joyful lives after they leave us.

Even when we understand this, some apprehension before an Ofsted is probably inevitable and may actually be healthy, with a complete indifference to Ofsted perhaps suggesting a certain arrogance. That said, there is no need for this to develop into all-consuming institutional panic, or for individual teachers to be swept up in it if this happens at their school.

Before appointment, it is possible to get some sense of whether the school is likely to be a stressful Ofsted experience by doing some research. Good, strong heads and SLTs are effective at managing a school's pre-inspection emotional charge. Clive Wright, the quietly inspirational head of St Martin's Catholic Academy in Stoke Golding, has banned the use of the word 'Ofsted' by SLT aside from in closed meetings because he feels this causes teachers to focus on trying to please them and not what is actually best for pupils. While, of course, Clive cannot (and I am sure does not) seriously police what his teachers talk about, I think he is right to try to create a culture that minimises unhelpful stress. Ensuring the focus remains on what's best for pupils – and not wasting time trying to second guess what inspectors want to see – means anxiety needn't become overbearing. This, obviously, is also the reason that schools preparing for inspection by running 'mocksteds' or 'reviews' are misguided: such activities increase anxiety, whip up fear and cause leaders and teachers to focus more on Ofsted ratings for their own sake rather than what is best for its pupils.

Plenty of schools do not indulge such in such nonsense and considerate, wise schools can be found in all areas. It is possible to identify them by looking at a range of indicators.

A good place to start, as Ofsted has now encouragingly acknowledged, is with the curriculum. If the school is running dubious qualifications (for example, in the past, the European Computer Driving License), it is likely that the school is game-playing and is more concerned with its external appearance and the Ofsted rating than what is best for its pupils. It is also worth reading the school's policies on planning, marking, teaching and assessment. Labour-intensive, over-prescriptive policies accompanied by a lot of monitoring might suggest the school's management is focused on visible compliance, which is another sign that leadership might be poorly managing its own anxiety about Ofsted. This anxiety may well spread to staff lower down the hierarchy.

While ideally it is best to work at a school with strong leadership and a positive attitude towards inspection, this is not always possible for everyone. Some teachers with personal responsibilities and commitments are tied to specific locations. Some will have commendable loyalty to the children and wider community at their schools and may not want to move, even when leadership is weak and the threat of inspection ever present. Even in these situations, however, there are things teachers can do to ensure they do not let the gloomy mood affect their own wellbeing.

When Franklin D. Roosevelt said, during the Great Depression, 'the only thing we have to fear is fear itself', he meant that the constant, soul-sapping dread caused by worrying about the worst possible outcome can actually become a self-fulfilling prophecy. If fear is not rationalised and managed, it can become all-consuming. This can be true of the schools which most fear Ofsted. In these places, Ofsted can assume a false villainy, as inaccurate rumours spread like knotweed. The most unscrupulous of heads, of which there are mercifully few, may even take advantage of this by spreading such disinformation in order to ensure compliance with their policies by, for example, claiming that Ofsted insists on seeing all work in children's books marked in depth.

Fortunately, I really do think things are changing. It has never been easier to find out if a directive comes from Ofsted or not. Ofsted genuinely appears to be trying to getting its house in order and has, commendably, made itself freely accessible to all teachers with a Twitter account. There is even a hashtag (#ofstedmyths), which means previously asked questions are easy to find. It is also helpful to remember, as described earlier in this chapter, that Ofsted has changed a great deal recently, and is continuing to change. Some of the aspects of inspection that most worried schools have been addressed and some of the fear that schools experience is based on years of accumulated anxiety more than it is the current state of play. If Ofsted is in the process of refining itself into a more effective and sophisticated organisation, as it hopes to be, there will be an inevitable and understandable lag time before schools trust that any changes are meaningful. The best thing teachers can do in the meantime is take Ofsted at its word and check their concerns are real.

Ofsted is scary enough as it is, and we should not believe or spread inaccurate rumours that make people even more afraid.

It is also important, however a school responds to Ofsted, that the teachers who work in said school keep the process and results of inspections in proportion. Within sensible, sustainable limits, teachers have a professional and moral duty to do their best for pupils; and what Ofsted says, whether positive or negative, really should not have any bearing on this. If we find ourselves doing things for Ofsted and not for the children we teach we are behaving unethically; and if a choice ever has to be made between what someone tells you Ofsted wants and the interests of your pupils, your pupils should win every time.

And even if the worst does happen, the outcome may not be anywhere as near as bad as you think it will be. As a wise older colleague once said to me, 'Yeah, it's horrible at the time. But they can't kill you. Or make your wife leave you. Or put you in prison. Or even sack you.'

A lesson in which you are observed may go really badly; but even if it does, remember this represents a minute slice of your practice as a whole and it would be entirely illogical to extrapolate any critique to your teaching in its entirety when you know what happened was out of the ordinary. This is, of course, hard. Very often, teachers wrap their sense of self-worth and identity up in their teaching, and to hear someone in a position of authority criticising this can hurt deeply, especially as it can feel like you've let the school down. No one individual can be held solely responsible for all the reasons a lesson goes badly. If the pupils behaved appallingly, for example, even if we leave aside the choices the children made, this is probably also a result of school culture for which the teacher cannot be held solely responsible. Teachers should remember this when receiving feedback and, while they should not automatically dismiss any advice, which might be helpful, they should avoid taking it personally and remember that there is always a context that the inspector is unaware of.

Teachers unlucky enough to suffer a rough inspection should also be aware that, by and large, they are almost certainly harder on themselves than their colleagues will be. In the raw moments after a bad experience, it is easy to fall victim to paranoia and believe everyone knows you messed up and is whispering in corridors and messaging over WhatsApp about your failure. This is probably not true. Firstly, Ofsted inspectors are not supposed to pass notes on individual lessons to anyone except the teacher they observed; and secondly, even if word does get out, by far the most common reaction is likely to be professional sympathy. If a colleague tells you their observation went badly, help them by downplaying it. Resist the temptation to go through a blow-by-bow post-mortem and, instead, shrug and ask them what they're doing at the weekend. Don't allow fear and paranoia the space to breathe.

Unfortunately it would be misleading to say that the absolute worst never happens. Sometimes Ofsted can trigger a witch-hunt, and some teachers may come under awful and unfair pressure afterwards. However, even if this does happen, it is still possible to retain a sense of proportion and dignity. Bullying happens in all sectors and we can help retain perspective by remembering that the working world beyond the school gates is no moral utopia. That said, we should also not forget that, most of the time, we have more options than we think we do while trapped in the maelstrom. Whether the result of Ofsted or not, if you find yourself bullied you should speak to your union. If you don't trust the union representative in your school, then ring the central office and get advice there. Or, a teacher's unique circumstances may make it sensible for them to avoid a scene and seek work elsewhere. Doing this is no failure and one advantage of the recruitment and retention crisis is that, in many subjects, those looking for a new job will probably not be without one for long.

While of course Ofsted can be scary, it is important to keep this fear in perspective. Inspections are comparatively rare and should not shadow day-to-day life, especially when their results are often far out of the control of teachers in classrooms. This is true even for schools operating in the most pressurised contexts. The sun rises again the morning after even the most awful of experiences. Your pupils and your duty to them hasn't changed. The colleagues you should most respect will understand. The weekend rolls around again. The people who love you still love you regardless; and if your situation becomes truly untenable, remember that your chances of finding a job elsewhere might well be better than you think.

The last Ofsted I underwent as a teacher and leader was horrible. But, in the last lesson of the second day of the inspection, while the inspectors and school SLT huddled together, a Polish girl who'd almost certainly never heard of Ofsted read aloud to the class for the first time and, unprompted, her classmates applauded her (Newmark, 2016). It was a big moment for all of us, just like the moment my whole class got 100% on a 50-question knowledge quiz for the first time, in a lesson I knew would never be observed. As unpleasant as any inspection process is, whoever's fault it is, the memories, moments and learning that last the longest will always be those forged in experiences completely unconnected to it.

If all seems lost, remember that.

Why is everything my pupils do wrong my fault?

I just had my appraisal. I was told that my first objective as a subject teacher was for all my pupils to reach their target grade. As a tutor, I have to make sure my form has 98% attendance. If they don't meet their targets, I might not get a pay rise next year. This seems totally unfair. I will teach as well as I can, but I can't control how hard the pupils revise or whether or not they concentrate properly in my lessons. And what if lots of parents of children in my form phone in and say they are poorly? Am I supposed to go to their houses and check if they are telling the truth? I said this to my line manager and they just accused me of 'making excuses'. When I ask other people what to do, they just tell me to 'log everything' so I can prove that I have tried. I feel like I'm doomed to fail and that the school is constantly trying to catch me out.

I was living abroad when I became responsible for the results of the first set of GCSE pupils I taught in my last school. Twenty-six years old and a brand-new VSO volunteer, I had no idea that somewhere on a different continent, 30 or so children were sitting SATs, and that their results would form the data on which, five years later, my ability as a teacher would be judged.

I wish someone had told me. If they had, I could have come straight home and done something to help. Unfortunately, nobody did; and by the time I took over this class – the year before their exam – it was too late. Most had done no meaningful history study at all while at secondary school and, despite my best efforts, they didn't do well. Perhaps it is actually for the best I remained in blissful ignorance. Even if had taught them for the last five years, how fair would it have been to ascribe their results solely to my teaching anyway?

For practical purposes, it doesn't matter how much we really contribute to the eventual grades our pupils get. Accountability and inspection mechanisms in

England have, until very recently, operated under the assumption that there is a direct correlation between teaching and pupil outcomes. If children do not do well in exams, unless a school and its teachers can make a really compelling case that teaching is good, it is assumed the school and teachers are to blame. Similarly, if attendance is low, this is attributed to the school's failure to plan strategies to get and keep children in the building. It often feels like nobody is allowed to challenge this narrative. Those who do speak up often find themselves shouted down with accusations of low expectations. High-performing schools find themselves in a much more comfortable position because it is assumed good results are solely due to their work.

This one-dimensional view of success and failure is, of course, nonsense.

Whether children do well or badly in their final exams, it is neither fair nor logical to hold their teacher solely responsible. Some children are tutored and others are not. Some may use online resources produced by other teachers. Some may be advantaged by parents who buy revision guides and insist on their use, while others have parents who don't see any point in school and will never purchase so much as a pen. Some have form tutors who phone home when homework is not done and some never encounter anyone who cares whether they bother or not.

And, of course, some children just try harder than others for reasons we don't understand and can't explain.

The truth is, a child's eventual result is the combination of a vast network of interlinking variables and any attempt to reduce it to a single one distorts the picture.

Even if the playing field could be levelled, which of course it can never be, teachers still should not be held wholly responsible because they do not have independence in their classrooms. Few (if any) teachers are free to plan, teach, assess, track progress or indeed do much of anything exactly how they want to. They must all follow policies they do not devise, good and bad, regardless of whether or not they agree with them. If a policy is a bad one – say, insisting a lesson begins with a discredited practice such as brain gym – it is not fair to blame only the teacher for disappointing results. Doing so provides fertile ground for micromanagement, invasive coercion and bullying as teachers are forced to do things they don't believe in, then blamed when these things don't work. For those teachers who absorb and accept the narrative it can also be soul-destroying, with those working in the most challenging circumstances coming to feel they are doing the worst job.

This nonsense would be much easier to ignore had so many schools not made it a key component of appraisals and associated performance-related pay. The fact that they have done so means there are thousands of teachers whose career, at least officially, is dependent on something over which they have limited influence. That so many think this is necessary to get teachers to work effectively is awfully depressing, and perhaps even dangerous. Motivating teachers with money or career advancement may lead to gaming systems, narrowed curriculums and cut corners more than it does better teaching. Teachers should do their best for pupils because it is a professional duty and moral responsibility, not for more cash, and to suggest otherwise is to slight the integrity of those who care very deeply. Furthermore, blaming teachers for the bad results of groups of children allows government and wider society to ignore important issues that actually have far more influence on underachievement.

Educating children is a community endeavour and, from the site team who fix the heating to the conscientious father reading to his child at night, we are all responsible. We could get someone to design a complicated algorithm that tries to work out exactly how much each teacher is accountable for each child's result. I'm sure this would please those with a love of spreadsheets who think numbers are the point. Or we could accept the blindingly obvious: this sort of bean counting is impossible, a waste of effort and damaging for recruitment and retention at a time we can't hire teachers or even keep the ones we have. Of course not all teachers are good enough and that shouldn't be ignored, but punishing teachers if children get poor exam results is a thoughtless way to deal with this.

Pointing out that the emperor isn't wearing any clothes is not making excuses or avoiding responsibility. It is telling the truth.

Understanding how and why we have come to this strange, illogical position takes some unpicking.

We blame teachers for so much because of a narrative that says that in the pre-Ofsted grammar-school era, they took no responsibility at all.

The story goes like this.

In the past, when there were plenty of manufacturing and primary industry jobs, it wasn't considered important whether most poorer children did well academically. Some brighter poorer children went to grammars where, benefiting from higher expectations, more highly qualified teachers and a more rigorous curriculum, they were equipped with the knowledge and skills needed to go to university and – if successful – were co-opted into the middle class.

The rest, making up the majority, went to secondary modern schools which taught mainly practical and functional skills and acted as holding pens until the young people in them were old enough to earn a wage. As children were (at least supposedly) selected for these different types of school by intelligence, a certain fatalism took hold: children at secondary moderns were, almost by definition, unintelligent. This meant that there seemed little point thinking much further about why they did not do well at school, making any attempt at improving standards of teaching a waste of time. The predominate view of secondary modern schools today is an overwhelmingly negative one. Whether it is Billy being bullied by his PE teacher in *Kes* or children being ground into sausages in the video for Pink Floyd's 'Another Brick in the Wall', the sense of hopelessness, misery and cruelty has become a powerful cultural trope.

This unnuanced view is unlikely to be accurate; but it makes no difference whether it is near the mark or a work of complete fiction. Much of the decision making of the last 30 or so years has been done under the assumption that schools for poor children were awful, and a reason for this was that most teachers in them didn't believe it possible for their pupils to do well academically, didn't try hard and were never held to account for poor performance because nobody cared.

In the 1970s and 1980s, as manufacturing and jobs in primary industry declined, attitudes towards education changed. Partly because new jobs in service industries were perceived as needing more white-collar-type skills, and partly because of a growing belief in more equality of opportunity and social mobility, governments began to take more of an interest in how poorer children were doing in school. This led to more investment which, quite rightly, led to more interest into how this was spent, whether it was having an effect and how standards could be improved.

Ofsted was created by John Major's Conservative government as part of the Education (Schools) Act of 1992 to investigate these things, with reports made public for parents, schools and government for the first time. While methods of inspection have shifted over time, the central premise has remained the same: schools are directly responsible for the results of their pupils and must improve themselves if judged to be substandard (Great Britain. *Education (Schools) Act 1992*).

The pressure applied by Ofsted was passed down from school management to rank-and-file teachers. The success of many once underperforming schools in London, often attributed to the London Challenge programme (Kidson and Norris, 2014), offered apparent proof that improvement was possible in even the most challenging of contexts, and that all that was getting in the way of wholesale national improvement was poor teaching and strategy, caused predominantly by the low expectations and dismissive attitudes of schools and the teachers in them. It was therefore believed that if schools outside London aped the methods used by those in it, they too would rapidly improve. While this explanation has been robustly challenged by researchers who have attributed much of London's improvement to other contextual factors, these challenges have been largely ignored by policy makers (Burgess, 2014).

This resulted in an even more bullish Ofsted. Michael Wilshaw, Her Majesty's Chief Inspector until 2017 and himself the ex-head of a successful school in London, was comfortable taking a confrontational approach when he thought it necessary, once famously saying, 'If anyone says to you that "staff morale is at an all-time low", you know you are doing something right' (Abrams, 2012). Politicians also adopted this line, with Michael Gove memorably referring to some teachers, educationalists, academics and unions as 'The Blob', and an obstruction to better outcomes, especially for poorer children (Garner, 2014).

These pressures created a strange, even cultish atmosphere in which seeking to explain any underachievement by looking at factors beyond teaching was, no matter how reasonable or thoughtfully expressed, just not acceptable. Those who tried to do so often found themselves silenced by accusations of 'low expectations', which became one of the most heinous offences of which a teacher could be accused. To those that persisted it was made very clear there was no place for even a discussion of such views; either accept the narrative or ship out. Finally, in 2010, this flawed view was formalised when the then education secretary, Michael Gove, abolished the contextual value added measure which had allowed comparison between schools experiencing similar challenges. The message was now clear and stark. Bad outcomes were now officially the result of bad schooling.

Although it isn't always easy to see, headteachers and senior leaders feel the pressure of accountability as much as their teachers do, and probably more so in many cases. Leadership and management is an area on which Ofsted grades schools, and to get a positive rating, leaders must demonstrate that they develop policies and strategies followed by all staff. Compliance with policy must be visible and, especially in schools at risk of a negative Ofsted judgement, this compliance can become more important than the quality of policy itself. The reason for this is quite logical: leaders who don't develop forceful policies – or are not able to ensure that their policies are followed – clearly are not effective, which on the face of it makes poor results a direct consequence of their incompetence. In these cases a negative overall judgement is likely to be supported by a negative leadership and management rating. Many SLTs spend little time or effort consulting widely or meaningfully before developing whole-school strategy and are rarely open to the suggestion that poor performance might be down to their policies. It is much easier for them to go along with the dominant narrative and assign blame for poor results to the poor teaching of individual teachers than it is to accept that their own decisions might be to blame.

The rise and rise of data in schools and the computer systems used to manage it has provided a new and powerful mechanism to continue to blame teachers. Now it is possible to grade a child multiple times a year in each subject and compare these figures to those of children at other schools and even between subjects in the same school. Spreadsheets are not good at dealing with issues that cannot be measured with a number and so these (as is culturally approved of) are ignored. The data – often of provenance that would horrify statisticians – is presented to teachers at appraisal to support judgements made about the quality of their practice.

Teachers at the bottom of the hierarchy in schools where children do not achieve good results can find themselves in something of a bind: they are held personally accountable for the results of their pupils without the agency to make significant changes, or the right to challenge the numbers even when they instinctively know they are being treated unfairly.

If all teachers and schools were judged as failing, it is likely objections would be louder; but by conditions inherent in the newest performance measure, they are not. By measuring achievement from a starting point and not the raw end grade, Progress 8 was supposed to be fairer for schools working in more disadvantaged areas and was warmly welcomed when it was first introduced. Under this measurement, schools are judged by how much progress children in a school make compared to children at other schools who started on the same SATs grades in English and Maths. If children in one school do better than the national average, the school is awarded a positive figure. If children do worse than the national average, the school is given a negative one. This means, by definition, that half of England's schools have a positive P8 score and half have a negative one. For those schools with a positive P8 figure, the conceit that progress is down only to the quality of the school is a very helpful one and it is quite rational not to challenge it. It is also understandable that leaders and teachers in high-performing schools do not always think too hard about the limitations of the data on which they are assessed. We all work hard and when this appears to pay off, it is unappealing to entertain the possibility that the results may not actually have that much to do with us.

Whether we are winners or losers, the P8 measure pits school against school and has failed, once again, to acknowledge the truth: no child is a clean slate. The reasons they perform comparatively poorly or comparatively well on their end-of-Year 6 tests do not evaporate when they walk through the gates of their secondary school. Wider contextual factors over which we have very little influence, wilfully ignored by accountability measures, will in many cases continue to affect the speed at which pupils learn.

Before making some suggestions as to how to cope with all of this, it is important to accept the good intentions behind the mistakes made, and that it is probable improvement can be at least partially attributed to greater accountability in a broader sense. While the bathwater may be murky, it might be unwise to throw it all out without acknowledging it may once have cleaned the baby.

If it is true that government was once unconcerned about the standard of academic education received by its poorest children, then the increased interest is a good thing. If it is true that teachers did not care for their pupils, or had too low expectations of their capabilities, then perhaps the intervention of Ofsted and increased emphasis on accountability was once beneficial. But even if this is accurate, things have gone too far. The idea that teachers should be solely held responsible for how their pupils do is a dangerous fiction and an obstacle to further educational improvement. Teachers have a duty to sow good seed regardless of the contexts in which they work; but to be fair we must recognise that not all fields are equally fertile. If we really insist on persisting with this wrongheaded belief, many teachers, quite understandably, will come to believe it is not worth working in the areas where they are needed the most.

What to do

There is an obvious answer. Those wanting the least stressful experience of how accountability works should teach in schools with the best exam grades, and ideally those with the highest Progress 8 scores. Teachers in these schools reap the benefits of the contextual advantages afforded to children in such areas. If you work in such a school, the good results achieved by the children in your classes will almost certainly be ascribed to your teaching and you will probably benefit – personally and professionally – from the consequences of this. It is important not to judge such teachers, who (by definition) make up around half the profession. Working in a struggling school and being blamed for disappointing results year on year – perhaps failing to achieve pay progression as a result, and living under the constant threat of a poor Ofsted – is exhausting. For many (perhaps most) wanting to work as teacher for a whole career, it is simply unsustainable. There is no shame in deciding this is not for you. I would, however, ask that those who do work in more advantaged schools be sensitive to the struggles of those who do not, and avoid viewing – or worse, describing – themselves as better practitioners because they happen to work in a place where fruit falls more easily from the tree.

Those teachers who, for whatever reason, work or want to work in schools where results are poor should not be automatically put off by the content of this chapter so far.

Most schools work in very challenging contexts, and many of those where results are comparatively poor take a pragmatic and sensible view of accountability. Even those that claim they hold teachers wholly responsible for outcomes may, in practice, be much more understanding. This is logical and probably necessary for the smooth running of a school. It is very rare for a school to achieve really great grades in one subject but not in another; and even when this does happen, differences between subjects make any direct comparison difficult. This means that were a school to rigidly stick to a policy in which no teachers would achieve a pay rise if results were poor when compared with national averages, in all likelihood this would mean awarding it to very few teachers in the school, if any at all, which would cause serious resentment, perceived unfairness and a turnover making effective management of the school impossible. In reality, capability procedures, pay rises and promotions are almost always at the discretion of the head. This means there is great variation in how accountability is actually applied to individual teachers. In some schools, including many which struggle, teachers are awarded pay rises almost automatically; others may make teachers provide evidence of their capability to justify an increment when pupil results are judged as weak.

Although in some schools lack of pay progression is common and a source of anxiety and stress, probably generally more typical is a sense of depression and inadequacy brought about by an unquestioning acceptance of the fallacy that teacher input is always equal to pupil outcomes. This happens because many teachers are not aware that the accountability measures on which they are judged are unfair and believe the narrative: good teachers get good results and bad teachers get bad ones. Those in this position can become deeply unhappy, feeling their own deficiencies are the reason their pupils underachieve and becoming even more depressed when any changes they make do not result in a dramatic transformation.

Learning the truth can actually feel like it makes things worse. The profession leans heavily on the cultural trope that great teachers change lives and many of us go into the classroom precisely for this reason. Films like *Dangerous Minds* and *Dead Poets Society* and recruitment campaigns in which children talk passionately about how individual teachers effectively saved them from a life of ignorant misery do nobody any favours. Accepting this might not be possible in the way we thought it was can cut away a sense of purpose, leaving teachers disillusioned and bereft.

For those searching for a renewed sense of meaning, philosophy can help. Purpose can be re-found in the belief that teaching is a moral duty, regardless of the outcome of it. Instead of teaching subjects so pupils will be rewarded by top marks, we should teach because teaching has value in itself. While exam results are important, they should not be the only purpose of education because when we make them so, beyond being the low-water mark against which the success of cleverer children is measured, educating those who fail becomes pointless.

By over-emphasising the result, we devalue the process – which should actually be the whole point.

While letting go of our egos means we can no longer reward ourselves for the achievements of the children we teach, it also frees us from the pointless and often paralysing guilt we feel when they do not do as well. Accepting that the influence of our roles is limited frees us from an exhausting cycle of self-congratulation and self-flagellation over things we have little control of because it, quite rightly, subordinates results to our moral obligation to teach as well as we can regardless of apparent success or failure. It allows us to focus on how to be better teachers in the broadest sense.

To use this as an excuse for fatalism or passivity would be very wrong. Viewing teaching as a moral duty rather than just a professional one actually makes it a much more serious, profound responsibility. It turns ignoring research on the most effective ways to teach into a moral error rather than just a professional one. It makes giving up on a child because we know they will fail the exam – or because they 'don't count' on P8 figures or because they are unpleasant – an actual ethical failure. It means the moral implications of a three-year Key Stage 4 must be discussed as well as what this will do to results. It means accepting that regardless of how small or large our influence and how successful or unsuccessful we are, our moral obligation remains a constant that cannot be ignored.

With this new sense of responsibility comes a renewed sense of privilege. While teaching has many frustrations (some inevitable and some infuriatingly unnecessary), being engaged in this important work should fill us with great pride. While we may argue about the best way to do it, or what it is fundamentally for, we agree that is right to educate children in schools. While sometimes we will enjoy it more than other times, and we may doubt our ability, or understandably decide the personal sacrifices are too much and leave the profession, we will never reach the end of our working lives and wonder whether the time we spent teaching was wasted on something that did not really matter. In almost every country in the world, schools breathe in children in the morning and breathe them out in the afternoon hoping that between the bells they will have learned to be more. Being a part of this noble enterprise is a wonderful thing.

So while nobody is wholly to blame for any perceived deficiencies in the results of their pupils, just as nobody is wholly responsible for great results, it shouldn't actually make any difference to how we approach our work.

Why is there always more work than it is ever possible to do?

I have been working at my new school for a few months now. The list of things I have to do is never-ending and there seems to be more to do every day. Just planning for my lessons takes hours and marking in the way the school want me to takes even longer. There are briefings every day before school and there are meetings three days a week after school. On the days when there aren't meetings, I have to run either detentions or intervention sessions for my exam groups. For my classes, I have to ring home to chase homework that isn't done; and for my tutor group, I have to contact parents about absences and behavioural concerns raised by other teachers. Everything I do has to be logged on the school computer system, which feels like it takes almost as long as doing it in the first place! No matter how many hours I work – and I am doing almost 60 a week – I never get it all done. As well as being really stressful, it also makes me feel so guilty because I am letting my pupils down. There's lots I like about being a teacher...but I don't think I can go on like this.

The flawed assumption that there is a direct and simple connection between what a teacher does and the outcomes of their pupils has led to the belief that the greater the volume of work, the better outcomes they will achieve on behalf of their pupils. If this were true then you could see how it might encourage a belief that the only morally justified cause of action for a teacher would be to sacrifice their own wellbeing on the altar of their pupils' future happiness. This kind of moral pressure doesn't exist in many other professions and helps support a narrative that those teachers wanting a life beyond their jobs are somehow letting children down.

When outcomes are judged to be poor, it can seem rational to those labouring under this misapprehension to believe that everything would be better if only teachers would work harder. Even when school leaders do acknowledge that their staff are already overworking, they often appear at a loss as to what to do about it. While it is common to talk about 'working smarter, not harder', it is far rarer to act on this sort of platitude meaningfully. Typically, school leaders are quick to add new tasks but much slower to eliminate them. The impossibility of saying definitively what is having (and what is not having) an impact makes it impossible to prove that anything has no effect. This makes stopping doing something feel scary, and risk-averse schools are far more comfortable adding new tasks than they are eliminating old ones.

Ambiguity over how long it is reasonable to expect teachers to work makes it difficult to discuss openly. While most are typically contracted for about 40 hours per week, they are implicitly expected to work far more than this. Few teachers object to this in principle, accepting it as an unspoken trade-off for the long holidays. It is this unspoken unacceptance that lies at the heart of the problem; the tacit nature of this agreement means there is rarely formal discussion as to how much more than contracted hours it is fair to expect staff to work.

The result has been an ever-increasing workload.

Surveys routinely show many to be working upwards of 60 hours a week, and bringing in a policy to cap time spent outside school might well mean many schools would have to fundamentally rethink the ways in which they operate (Richardson, 2016).

Of the factors leading to unsustainable workload, the fetishisation of marking is certainly among the most significant. Not too long ago, the thought of a teacher providing extensive individual comments on hundreds of exercise books every fortnight would have been considered ludicrous, whereas now this is widespread. Some schools go even further and expect teachers to comment on adaptations children have made to their work based on a first round of marking, doubling the load at a stroke. These double- or even triple-marking policies, sometimes described as 'dialogic', expect teachers to engage in written conversations with all their pupils in addition to grading and offering suggestions for improvement. This overemphasis on written feedback, despite no evidence that this leads to faster learning (Aubrey, 2016), was partially driven by Ofsted reports which praised schools with such policies (*And All That Blog*, 2016) and a direction that 'children should have the opportunity to respond to feedback'. Although Ofsted has replied and have now stated explicitly they do not expect to see any particular style or volume of marking, many schools, probably because the practice has become so well established, have yet to act (Independent Teacher Workload Review Group, 2016).

Perhaps just as insidious was the phenomenon of 'child-centred learning', which was adopted by many schools and helped form criteria on which Ofsted inspectors – and schools in response – judged teaching. Many schools and teacher training providers interpreted the well-intentioned concept of differentiation to mean setting different tasks to groups and individuals within one class. A belief took hold that in order to meet children's individual needs, good teachers developed their own personalised resources for every lesson and avoided one-size-fits-all resources, such as textbooks, as these, written by people who did not know the pupils who would use them, could never meet the needs of unique individual children. The effect of this was a huge increase in workload as teachers became expected to produce plans and resources for multiple lessons within each of their timetabled slots.

Teachers who did not do this could be accused of failing to meet the needs of their pupils and could be reprimanded or even dismissed. While child-centred learning, at least interpreted in the way I have described, is no longer as widespread, its legacy is still felt in many schools.

Professor Becky Allen's lecture on 'Making teaching a job worth doing (again)' (Allen, 2017) offers some valuable insights on other winds that contribute to the perfect storm of teacher workload. Allen links recent increases in workload to significantly increased school budgets during the New Labour years. Many headteachers chose to spend this money on expanding management in general and senior teams in particular, with the aim of strengthening leadership. In order to justify their new positions, those appointed set others tasks which had not existed before. While some of these tasks might well have been worthwhile, in many schools this resulted in unrealistic expectations of how much work could – and should – be done by teachers. Allen also points out an unintended consequence of protecting non-contact time. Before non-contact time was specifically protected, school leaders knew there was little space in which teachers could complete additional tasks, and this may have made them more sensitive about setting them. Protected time allowed leaders the illusion that teachers had the capacity to do more non-teaching work. If there had been more thought on how much could realistically be done in the extra time then things may not have turned out as they did. But there was not. Instead, the new cups were filled so often and by so many people that soon they were overflowing. Allen quotes a teacher as saying:

> The day they gave me that time they made it management's business how I planned, how I prepared, and how I assessed. Because it was timetabled, it was now legitimate for a headteacher to ask me to do **anything** in that time. And they didn't just ask for **anything**, they asked for **everything**.

Working with data can be just as time consuming. Fifteen years ago, data collection, input and analysis in the modern sense was virtually unknown because the capacity to work with it did not exist in schools. As hard as it is to imagine now, there was a time – pre the digital revolution – before there was a market for school-management software. Instead teachers looked at grades and scores hand-recorded in mark books, which they would look over before writing reports or seeing parents. Things have certainly changed. Now most teachers are expected to enter a grade into a spreadsheet at least every term (and commonly even more often than that) for every child they teach. They are then often expected, flying in the face of all statistical literacy, to break down their classes into micro-cohorts and write reports on how these groups are doing compared to the rest of the class. These are not quick tasks and it is important to acknowledge that before school data tracking systems, they weren't done at all. An entirely new order of tasks has been created and little, if anything, has been removed to compensate. Every minute spent working on a computer with data is a minute of work that did not exist 15 years ago. This is not to go so far as to say that the proliferation of data has brought no value to schools at all, but any good it has brought has come with a cost and this, paid by teachers, has rarely been acknowledged. This is something Jo Facer, an English teacher and vice principal, wrote about in her widely shared blog post 'At what cost?', in which she concluded that even if her efforts to spot and then act upon underperformance had resulted in faster pupil progress, the ends did not justify the means:

> If I knew I would have to run intervention in this way until retirement, would I stay in this profession? Absolutely not. Do I want to stop running intervention and instead delegate it to my team, asking them to similarly give up weekends and holidays? Absolutely not. (Facer, 2015)

And all this new data, for any good it might bring, has had detrimental effects on the way schools run too. Carl Hendrick, in his blog post (Hendrick, 2015) on how the US lost the war Vietnam because it made the mistake of measuring success or failure on body count (an error now widely known as the McNamara fallacy – see the chapter 'Why is everyone so scared of Ofsted?'), points out that the domination of numbers and letters can easily lead to undue value being placed on what can be measured – at the expense of important things which cannot. In many schools, it has become more important for numbers to go up than to consider what these numbers actually represent. Student performance in most subjects simply can't be reduced to one figure without significant distortion of the curriculum. This has created a situation in which the work teachers do is actually made less meaningful by the assessment systems in which they have to operate. For example, a teacher forced to assess children in Year 7 against a GCSE rubric designed to assess them at the end of Year 11 is, as Daisy Christodoulou explains in *Making Good Progress?*, unable to focus on the constituent building blocks of final performance (Christodoulou, 2017). This would be comparable to a football coach tasked with improving results, but only being allowed to record progress by noting the number of goals scored. Good teachers know this to be nonsense, so many personally record more-meaningful data that is never officially logged, further increasing workload.

When it becomes clear that children are unlikely to meet a predetermined set standard, emphasis can quickly shift from genuinely helping them improve to creating evidence that their failure to hit the target is not the fault of their school or the teachers working in it. Volume of work – the more the better – becomes the focus. Instead of planning teaching sequences to build on existing knowledge and understanding, teachers spend time pointlessly gathering and logging evidence of tasks they have done so that disappointing results cannot be attributed to their own laziness or passivity. This can soon become a painful, exhausting process: a child does not complete homework, so a phone call has to be made to parents; nobody answers and this has to be logged; the parent must be phoned again and again, each attempt logged to prove the teacher did it; eventually contact is made and a parent is asked to come to school for the umpteenth time that year; a meeting is arranged (even though nobody really thinks it will make any difference) just so it can be logged as evidence that something has been done.

While it would be too cynical to say the only cause of the rise of time-consuming after-school, weekend and holiday 'interventions' is to provide evidence that all that can be done has been done, it has certainly been a contributing factor. These interventions, once unheard of, are now typical practice. Whether or not they have any positive impact on learning, these increase timetables by stealth because they are rarely if ever included in an assessment of a teacher's directed hours. In many cases, such interventions become extra lessons after school – sometimes even called period 6 – done with no extra pay or preparation time. Schools skating around the ethics of this by claiming such programmes are voluntary should consider how a junior member of staff who refuses to give up their time in this way is likely to be regarded by their line manager and colleagues. For many, such activities feel compulsory even if the school describes them as voluntary.

Schools are not entirely to blame for this. The largely cohort-referenced nature of GCSE and A level examinations means that children (and, by association, schools) are in competition with each other. This means that those schools who do not provide extra tuition for their pupils are quite logical to fear being outcompeted by those that do (Enser, 2017).

In the past, when there were more older and more experienced teachers, such changes might have encountered more resistance. The changing, increasingly young nature of the teaching profession has resulted in little formal objection to this increase in workload, which has normalised longer hours. Now, in some schools, few teachers remember a time when very long workdays and weekend work weren't typical. Younger teachers, on the whole, have fewer non-work commitments. Keen to impress and get ahead, they are also more willing and able to complete large volumes of work. Being cheaper, too, they are understandably attractive to school leaders working with increasingly constrained budgets. This can very easily create a culture in which working weeks of 60 hours or more are simply accepted as an inevitable part of the job.

It could, of course, be argued that, from an educational standpoint, this is not a problem so long as there are plenty of new recruits to replace those who, on acquiring other commitments, find their job no longer sustainable and move on. Indeed, one young senior leader told me recently that pensions and workload didn't concern her because teaching was not a career anyone really expected to do beyond their early thirties. Even if issues around teaching quality caused by predominantly inexperienced staff are put to one side, it is becoming more and more apparent that there simply aren't enough people training to be teachers to replace those that leave. This may well be because for every young person inspired by the idea of teaching there are many more who quite understandably fail to see the appeal of working stockbroker hours for wages that have, in real terms, declined by 12% over the last ten years (Weale, 2017). This may well have kickstarted a vicious cycle in some schools; fewer teachers in schools, whether young or older, means more work for those that remain, which further increases pressure and leads to even more departures.

High turnover has also increased the number of comparatively young senior leaders. Whereas once a teacher with five years of experience was regarded as still having plenty to learn, now in some schools this is sufficient for a successful appointment to an assistant or even deputy head role. Such people, accustomed to working very long hours themselves and perhaps still without significant non-work commitments that make such a pattern unsustainable in the long term, may hold this as an expectation of others. Older, more experienced SLTs, having gained their experience in an era before the issues described in this chapter fully took hold, may well not understand the implications of the policies they develop and enforce because it is difficult to fully understand the work involved in, say, entering and analysing data or marking books for a full timetable of classes when you have never had to do this yourself.

Of course senior leaders have their own pressures. Changes to the format of Ofsted inspections has made their jobs much more stressful and time consuming than previously. Until 2005, Ofsted inspected schools for a week at a time every six years, and schools were given two months to prepare. This made for very busy periods in which schools had to get their houses in order. The move to shorter, two-day inspections with only 24 hours' notice should, on the face of it, have improved matters as schools no longer had so long to prepare, limiting the pinch points.

Things did not work out this way. Changes to the structure of inspections placed more emphasis on SLTs having a firm grasp of the strengths and weaknesses of their schools, which made them hungry for information from those lower in the hierarchy. This created lots more report writing and record keeping and even, in some schools, an insistence that planning is handed in each week to be checked. This hunger for information is also, at least partially, responsible for the rise and rise of quality assurance, which means teachers can feel as if they are constantly under scrutiny, which is deskilling, demoralising and demotivating because it removes agency from teachers, making it their job simply to follow the directions of their supposed superiors. In effect, the high-stakes nature of inspection (explored in the chapter 'Why is everyone so scared of Ofsted?') understandably led to heads, and the teams below them, placing their schools on permanent battle alert, as the volume of work needed as evidence of good management simply could not be produced in the 24 hours after The Call. In reality, instead of reducing workload, the change in format has increased it because schools now have to be prepared for a visit at all times.

Launched in 2019, Ofsted's latest framework, which puts a much greater emphasis on curriculum, will almost certainly increase workload in the short term for many schools, who will not only have to make sure that their curriculum is strong but also find ways to demonstrate this.

These perverse incentives are perfectly predictable. Each addition to workload has been the result of individuals and groups making decisions that are entirely logical in the contexts in which they work. If outside pressures were tackled thoughtfully, and the context made more conducive, then workload should decline and move to a more sensible, sustainable level. Or so the argument goes. In reality, even making big structural changes may not lead to significant reductions in the hours teachers work because of one very powerful interest group: teachers themselves, who sometimes have only themselves to blame.

For whatever reason, the image of the heroic teacher dragging their flu-ridden body into school for half six, and then working late into the evening six days a week is a widely cherished cultural trope, reinforced by TV shows such as the Channel 4 series *Educating...* and the more recent *School* on BBC Two. It can be seen in vacuous, dangerous inanities shared on social media such as 'A good teacher is like a candle. It consumes itself for others.' This nonsense is not, of course, limited to teachers. Nurses, social workers and paramedics also suffer from it too. As a culture, it sometimes feels like we want our public servants to martyr themselves for the greater good, with exhaustion the proof of how much they care. It is also possible this idealisation of those in caring, compassionate jobs allows a certain societal indifference to the long hours they work; if someone is regarded as some sort of superhuman, then superhuman effort and sacrifice can be reasonably expected of them. Additionally, the sentimental fetishisation of childhood means that teaching young people is viewed as a privilege so profound that those lucky enough to do it are expected to cheerfully complete all manner of unnecessary tasks, irrespective of how tangentially the work is connected to learning. Those complaining about double-marking policies or death by meaningless data can find themselves shut down with a condescending smile and comments along the lines of 'Oh, but it's worth it for the kids', as if pointless, aimless administration and exhausting drives for consistency are a fair price to pay for the unadulterated joy inevitably derived from working with young people. Teachers who don't feel comfortable describing their jobs in such emotive terms and prefer to speak in more measured, professional tones can find themselves looked at with a degree of suspicion and distrust.

If such nonsense was limited to fiction and we indulged in it in the same way we appreciate the romantic presentation of cowboys in westerns, it probably wouldn't do much damage. Dangerously, though, this naive idealism has been appropriated by some policy makers and unscrupulous or unthinking schools leaders. It has also been swallowed wholesale by many rank-and-file teachers who use it to torture themselves and those unfortunate enough to have to work with them.

Like Japanese salarymen conspicuously sleeping at their desks, teachers who believe this compete with each other over the amount of work they do and take pride showing that they do more than their colleagues. Whether they do this because they genuinely believe it helps their pupils, out of insecurity or to impress those higher in the pecking order, the results are invariably destructive.

Double marking is doubled, pretty images adorn resources framed by colourful borders and piles of marking are photographed and shared on social media, sometimes with annoying emojis and daft hashtags.

Such unseemly virtue signalling is most damaging for those early in their careers who haven't yet developed a strong sense of their own identities as teachers. These unfortunates can very easily come to believe they must match or even exceed such herculean levels of effort. Nobody benefits from this arms race. Even those willing and able to keep up are likely to find, sooner or later, there comes a time when even they cannot sustain such a punishing regimen and fail at the standards they established for themselves. For those who know no other way, this can cause huge anxiety and stress, and for some it will end promising careers. Others, unwilling for whatever reason to compete, may leave teaching before they've hardly begun. A final effect of this is the emergence of a 'shape up or ship out' mentality, which means those that remain have fewer and fewer colleagues working manageable hours to act as role models, normalising overwork even further.

Not too long ago, teaching unions acted as a buffer. New policies – or adaptations to existing ones – which added to workload might once have resulted in a union meeting within a school which could, at least potentially, lead to industrial action. While this was very rare, the possibility made school leaders more careful and thoughtful when introducing a new idea or strategy. Union representatives could also act informally, perhaps speaking to a young staff member about how doing too much undermines their colleagues. Indeed, in my second year of teaching, after I wrote almost a page for each child's annual report, this happened to me. While it is possible that unions got in the way of some necessary reform, the decline in their influence may well have done more harm than good overall, as the spiralling of workload is almost certainly a significant cause of the problems in recruitment and retention which now undermine the quality of England's education system as a whole. If this is true, it is a shame that teaching unions have been unable to maintain influence in the face of far-reaching and profound changes that appear to have left them much diminished in many schools.

There is no simple answer as to why teachers have to work so hard, often for little gain for either themselves or their pupils. A combination of connected factors is to blame, which makes doing anything about it tough and, for individual teachers, even tougher. That said, the situation is not hopeless. There are many, many teachers who have found ways to make workload manageable and thrive. In the next part of this chapter, I hope to describe how this might be made possible.

What to do

Those looking for a new job should do research and find a school with a sensible approach. Schools vary and many do take meaningful steps to make workload manageable. Before applying for a position, contact the school and ask for copies of their policies. If these demand fortnightly double marking of all work or that teachers run all their own detentions, then this probably means very long hours. If a school is evasive or, worse, flatly refuses to provide such information, this is a telling sign, and by not choosing to apply, you may well be dodging a bullet. If policies aren't clear, ask to speak to someone, preferably within department, to get a proper picture. Be wary of platitudes such as 'We value work-life balance' and grand gestures like locking up the school building at a certain time, because these, on their own, will not result in an overall reduction in working hours. If a school values its staff and is genuinely committed to their wellbeing, then such inquisitiveness is likely to be welcomed, and by asking questions you may even do yourself a favour as it shows you to be thoughtful and proactive. Schools that take a dim view of such questions are likely to be ones in which you would not want to work anyway. Ideally, if possible, try to speak informally to teachers already at the school. This is easier for those living locally, but even those who do not may be able to subtly use social media networks to find and talk to existing staff. While this may feel a little furtive, it is better viewed as sensible due diligence: all you are doing is finding out what it is like to work somewhere that will have a huge influence over your personal and professional happiness and satisfaction.

Teachers should also be aware that what is stated as an expectation does not always reflect the reality on the ground. One of the hardest things about starting a new job is not being able to distinguish between tasks that absolutely must be done and those that officially should be done but are, in practice, tokenistic. The problem here is that school policy documents often imply that everything is high priority and those in management positions are unable, for obvious reasons, to communicate the nuances. This can make a new job utterly exhausting even for experienced teachers. It is probably wise to accept that, in the short term, workload will be higher than normal. At the beginning, more so than at any other point, it is important to try to do everything to establish your own professionalism beyond doubt and to create a positive impression that will make everything else easier in the longer term. Having a strong reputation makes it easier to find and speak to trusted peers, to work out how long each task is taking teachers who've worked at the school for a while, and to ask for examples of the planning, marking, reports, analysis and other tasks they are submitting. It may well turn out that while, on the face of it, a task such as analysing data for all your classes takes hours and hours, it is done much more concisely by other teachers in much less time, and this is regarded as quite acceptable by the school.

It might also be helpful to take stock of your own planning, teaching and assessing habits to see if there is fat that can be cut. Some teachers, particularly those trained in the context of child-centred learning, may well be doing more than is necessary because they know no other way. Here, time invested in getting up to date with the current context and educational research may well pay off. It may well turn out that time-consuming tasks once considered essential – such as producing different versions of a worksheet for different students in one class, or spending long hours making an Anglo-Saxon version of *Monopoly*, or populating a *Guess Who?* template with Shakespearean characters – may not be necessary or actually even desirable. Doug Lemov's 'hurdle rate' can act as a useful guide here: if the objectives of any activity can be more efficiently met by reading, then perhaps the activity should be reconsidered regardless of how exciting or superficially engaging it is. This can, of course, be painful, as it might mean recognising that a significant proportion of a career has been spent planning tasks that had no real benefit. Teachers in this position shouldn't feel too bad about it. Professionals change their views when evidence changes and don't take challenges to their methodology personally. Those choosing to spend hours on jobs that aren't necessary should, at the least, not moan about workload and should take steps to make sure those around them do not feel they should be doing the same.

There are often significant reductions that can be made to time spent assessing. For all the mistakes they have made in the past, Ofsted is firmly in support of this. In 2016, they updated their instructions to inspectors to make it clear they did not expect any specific volume of marking to be completed and, in the absence of firm research showing that extensive written feedback makes any difference to learning, told their inspectors not to attribute any level of progress to it (Aubrey, 2016).

Teachers should, politely and constructively, make sure that their managers are aware of this and should not be afraid to suggest alternatives. Recently, a great deal of work has gone into verbal feedback, which takes a lot less time and, done well, may actually lead to faster progress.

It can also be helpful audit your own working patterns. One of the biggest time-sappers is 'half-work', when teachers try to accomplish too many things at once. Doing this includes working in front of the TV or after school with friends, when general discussion about the day and sharing funny things children have written in tests can easily become more of a focus than the actual task in hand. This makes everything take longer and also results in lower quality work overall. It probably isn't fair for those who work like this a lot to complain about the hours they're putting in until they've at least tried being more efficient with their time.

Unfortunately, not all teachers have the freedom to make significant changes to their working habits because in some schools these are prescribed by management as 'non-negotiables'. As an aside, management in such schools should, if they are unwilling for whatever reason to be less controlling, avoid saying 'Work smarter!' when confronted with the workload implications of their decisions because, without agency, this is as impossible as it is irritating to hear.

Those working in schools with unreasonable expectations of workload should not automatically assume that nothing can be done to reduce it. It is easy to forget that behind what might appear a monolithic, unfeeling work-generating machine sit human beings, and that vanishingly few of these take malicious glee in making teachers miserable, exhausted and perpetually anxious. Sometimes, workload spirals simply because those in charge of setting work do not know just how much chalkface teachers are doing because, being responsible for only part of the puzzle, they lack the big picture. Even teachers who suspect the school is fully aware of just how hard they are working might be wise to proceed in good faith in order to avoid creating the defensiveness that might cause a shutdown of communication which makes any change at all impossible.

A good start is to keep an itemised diary, or audit, of all the work you are doing over a half-term period. This should break down what is done each day and the total time it took to do everything. Make sure this is an honest, accurate reflection of reality and, no matter how tempting it may be to do so, don't exaggerate it to make a point. Sometimes just the act of keeping a record flags up inefficient patterns of work which can then be streamlined. If the diary does show a very high volume of work, then share it with line management in a scheduled meeting and ask if the hours you work are acceptable and, if not, seek suggestions on how the load could be reduced to a working week both you and your manager agree is reasonable. It can also be helpful to have solutions of your own, but these shouldn't be shared until managers have a chance to act and should be phrased in a way that reflects the priorities behind policies; ranting about the pointlessness of a strategy and asking for it to be eliminated is unlikely to be well received even if you are in the right. Act on any suggestions and see if they make a meaningful difference. If they do not, politely ask for a meeting with someone higher in the food chain. At all costs, avoid making this seem like a trap; make it clear that you aren't moaning for the sake of it, but are genuinely trying to find a way to make your load sustainable for the good of both yourself and the school. It is also important to avoid being emotional, as this can feed into a narrative that you aren't coping, which can result in patronising suggestions like mindfulness or other stress-management programmes which treat only the symptoms and not the causes of overlong hours.

There is, of course, no guarantee of success. If, after trying this, there is no improvement, difficult choices will have to be made. Some teachers may think it worth going all the way to governors, which might have an impact; while others may rightly feel they have no choice but to either put up with it or look for employment elsewhere. Whichever of these options teachers choose, it is important to continue completing all tasks as far as is possible until there is a successful resolution to protect professional reputations and, potentially, references.

Teachers should also be mindful of the impact of visible overwork on others. As discussed earlier in this chapter, hours spent resourcing, creating beautiful PowerPoints or writing ten-page reports when others write only one normalises heavy workloads for everyone and raises the bar too high for many perfectly competent teachers. Of course, for many teachers, these activities are pleasurable and it would not be fair to say all those making really pretty worksheets are doing their colleagues a disservice. That said, such teachers should recognise that they are more of a personal hobby than a professional obligation and should be open about this, in the same way that those teachers choosing to spend their own time at research conferences and TeachMeets should not expect everyone to give up personal time. We should also recognise that careers should be marathons (not sprints), that we are all likely to have times when we can do more and times when we have to do less, and that here should be enough flex in the system to accommodate this.

Above all else, regardless of how many hours they are working, teachers should not contribute to higher workloads by pretending they are managing when they aren't or by undermining others by virtue signalling their own overwork. When teachers are directed to overwork, they should make this clear, and that they are unhappy about it.

Nobody sees us at our desks at home as the clock rolls over the hours. Nobody sees the tensions that build up as those closest to us pick up the slack we are either too busy or exhausted to reel in ourselves. We alone see our hobbies and interests quietly die through neglect until we half-forget we ever played in a band or read novels in the evenings. All managers and colleagues see is that the work is done and we seem to be coping, right up to the point where we either spectacularly melt down or shuffle away from our profession never to return. When we make work invisible, it becomes unquantifiable, allowing the system the plausible deniability to say 'We didn't know they were working so hard. They should have said.'

So long as this continues, there will be no end. So long as the trees are taken home and uncomplainingly beavered away at, the system will keep adding more.

We should not cloud the issue by saying things like 'If I'm marking in front of the TV, it doesn't feel like work so I don't mind' if there are really other things we'd rather be doing. And we shouldn't say 'Education conferences are so much fun, I don't see them as work' if we are directed there against our will. If you are working, you are working. If it feels like you never do anything but work, say so politely – but loudly and clearly too. Do not hide the work you do. Make it so visible that nobody can pretend there isn't a problem. Be vocal about what you are doing and what you missed to get it done. Try saying, with a sad, disarming smile, 'Yes, I did the data analysis on Saturday morning while my partner took the kids swimming. I should have taken them myself, but this meant I couldn't, and that really upset me.'

So, as a final plea, make the work visible. If it means fewer of us leave teaching, doing less is in the interests of everyone – most of all, the children we teach.

Why won't my pupils work hard?

It is the Easter holiday, and I'm panicking about my Year 11 GCSE group. They did badly in their mocks and most of them didn't seem to care. They openly tell me they don't revise. Some have even said they may not bother to show up for their final exams. I've tried everything to motivate them – from detentions and phone calls home, to bribing them with chocolate for doing homework – but nothing really seems to work. I keep telling them how important these exams are for their future lives, but they just shrug and say things like 'Not bothered' or 'Do I look like I care?' Some of them are quite cheerful about it all and seem perfectly happy to leave school with hardly any qualifications. I am at my wits' end. I work so hard preparing lessons and revision resources for them but it all feels so one-sided. Why don't they care as much as I do?

Teachers with concerns like this are more likely to be working in disadvantaged state schools than they are to be in private schools or schools in affluent areas. While every school in the country will have at least some unmotivated pupils, the sort of mass disaffection alluded to here is always more common in poorer areas than it is in richer ones.

The most common explanation given for this is 'low aspirations', which means that pupils in the poorest areas do not work hard because they do not ever expect to be in contexts in which academic success is necessary.

There is logic to this. Pupils who attend schools in which few children go on to A levels or university and in areas in which many go straight into unskilled work may well struggle to see the significance of good exam grades. Children who do not know anyone who has gone on to become a teacher, doctor, lawyer or architect may see these sorts of destinations as unrealistic for them, making the pathways to get there seem irrelevant.

This explanation is the reason many schools spend money, time and effort on explicit attempts to 'raise expectations'. Such programmes typically involve external speakers, mentoring, and trips to universities and workplaces.

If this were the whole truth then improving pupil motivation would be simple. To motivate pupils, just show them the sunlit uplands that good results unlock.

This argument assumes that those who do not work hard in school make the choices they do out of a sort of dumb witlessness: because they know nothing about what it is like to reap the rewards of hard work, they are lazy. If (the argument goes) they can be shown how much better their lives would be if they took advantage of the opportunities afforded to them, they will work harder and achieve more. The job of career services, schools and teachers should be to lift the veil of ignorance and by so doing dispel the false consciousness that leads poor and underachieving children to assume that all is well when it really is not.

But if things really were as simple as this then surely schools should be more successful than they are?

Sadly, most evidence seems to suggest that if an aim of education is social mobility, we are failing: high-income professions remain as dominated by the middle and upper classes as they ever have been. One explanation for the failure of 'raising aspirations' initiatives to deliver wholesale change might be that visits to dreamy ancient universities or modern buzzy open-plan tech company offices seem about as authentic, realistic and relatable as going to the moon to children who feel culturally distant from them. Taking some pupils to these destinations may actually be counterproductive because it can confirm their belief that they would never fit in there.

The problem here is the value judgement made when we think this way: we are assuming that there is something wrong with children who do not aspire to attain academic qualifications and go on to study at university. We frame them as problems requiring solutions, which is certainly not the way in which most superficially unmotivated children see themselves.

Many apparently disaffected young people often tell us that they don't care about gaining qualifications because they are quite happy as they are and don't want to change. Rather than immediately dismiss this out of hand, it would be fairer to at least consider the possibility this is a truth we should respect and try to understand.

We might begin by examining what those often perceived to be lazy do with their free time.

Although there are some children who actually do nothing, there are actually relatively few. Most do have interests they happily devote time and effort to – going to the gym, mountain biking, anime, computer games, parkour, or something else.

It is usually not that they are unwilling to work at anything at all, but more that they are unwilling to do the things we think they should.

Of course, this can be even more frustrating; and it is easy to reflexively ascribe the blame for this to children, their parents, or the contexts in which they live. Schools can be too quick to assume that the diet they offer children is self-evidently good for them and that their resistance is based on an ignorance which must be overcome. In effect, what we are often saying is 'You may not like your greens – in fact you may be allergic to them – but we know they're good for you so we'll force you to eat them whether you want to or not.'

We hope that short-term pain will result in longer-term gain.

One barrier to this is expecting children to sacrifice their immediate happiness for a longer-term goal which may or may not ever come true. This is often just not realistic. Childhood is an all-encompassing state of being with those in it finding its end as hard to comprehend as adults do their own deaths.

I remember feeling this very keenly as a boy of about 11 when I moved from a local primary school connected to my church to a middle school some distance away. Here, for the first time, I felt different. I was different. It was a predominantly working class school...and I was not predominantly working class. The other children already knew each other well; I didn't know anybody. I went to church every Sunday. Few other children there did. Quickly labelled 'posh', I was mimicked and laughed at. For a while, I was very down; and knowing that this upset my parents, I kept quiet about it. But there were tears. I stopped working as hard at school because I felt that 'clever', on top of all the other things that marked me out as atypical, was a label I was better off without. I became obsessed by football – now I think about it, this was not really out of genuine interest but because I knew this was what the other boys liked, and I thought learning enough about it might be the key that led to acceptance and contentment. I do not share this story for sympathy. I would be a fool to. My privileges have in the long run predictably turned out to be enormous assets – educationally, financially, professionally and personally too. But as a child I didn't recognise this – and nor would I have cared if I had. My school life was miserable and I would have done anything to be happier. The idea that by working hard I was more likely to be a successful adult one day (and should take comfort from this abstract thought) was inconceivable to me because the immediate world I lived in was all I knew and the idea of 'growing up' had very little meaning.

As vivid as my memories are of this time, I'm well aware that any comparison between my experience and those of most pupils living in circumstances conventionally described as disadvantaged is flawed – not least because working hard at my school wasn't typical, my parents were doctors, I lived in a home full of books and I spent holidays visiting museums and art galleries. Although for a while all this felt like a disadvantage, it did mean that the world of academic success was one in which I unconsciously knew I belonged.

Michael Merrick, the deputy headteacher of a school in Cumbria, has done a lot of thinking on why this might not be true for many young people (Merrick, 2017). He argues that the values, language and behaviours deemed most desirable by schools and other academic institutions are often at odds with those of the communities from which their pupils come. If being 'academic' means reading different newspapers, speaking in a different accent, having different political beliefs or watching different sports from your friends and family, it may well be entirely reasonable to decide that the price of co-option into a different class and way of life is not worth paying. And, while it may be possible for some to move between different worlds, those attempting this are vulnerable to feeling like imposters in both.

Effectively we are asking many young people to give up their own identity and assume another – and to risk having no identity at all if this fails.

This is often not well understood by teachers and schools. Generally, those involved in education are from contexts in which university is, if not taken for granted as part of growing up, at least normalised. Teaching is a graduate profession, which means every fully qualified teacher went to university. This creates a palpable empathy gap between those responsible for dispensing education and those receiving it. Many teachers are unable to understand why anyone wouldn't want to go on to higher education – and many of their pupils are equally baffled as to why anyone would want to.

Some children do not work anywhere near as hard as teachers think they should because they simply do not want to become what their teachers want them to be and may well have very good reasons for this.

This effect is even more pronounced when what teachers want their pupils to be and how they want them to act clashes with a child's deeply held sense of identity. Children from backgrounds in which academic success is neither common nor valued may have other goals which are very important to them. For example, such children may derive immense and understandable satisfaction from being a caring sibling, a good footballer, a vivacious party animal or a cheeky and popular local character. Achieving good grades at school and the work necessary to get these might be perceived to be in direct opposition to a child's goals because studying hard can mean not doing other things from which identity and self-worth are constructed.

This also rolls into behaviour in classrooms. If children are not motivated by the rewards their teachers think they should be, then it is easy to understand why they might not properly engage with learning. Making funny comments, acting the goat to amuse classmates or building status through calculated defiance might well seem a better use of their time.

Comparatively recent changes to the way we justify education as a society may well have made motivating and interesting pupils harder than it once was. New Labour's well-intentioned focus on 'education, education, education', made an increase in the overall number of children going on to further education a key success measure. This may have unintentionally de-emphasised the inherent value of the content taught because it inadvertently implies that the only point of it all is the destinations pupils go on to after leaving their schools. If pupils think the only point of school is further education, and they don't want to do this, then what is the point of trying? The recent changes to GCSEs and the language around them used by government has also not helped. Identification of grade 4 as a pass means anything lower is a de facto fail, which reinforces the impression that if a child cannot achieve a passing grade, their lessons are a waste of their time.

Unintentionally, recent changes have created and then strengthened a culture that makes the content of academic subjects seem rarefied and exclusive.

A world for posh, clever people. Not our world.

Not for the likes of us.

What to do

The point of education has not always been exam results and going to university. In the past, more value was placed on the inherent value of what was taught and its ability to culturally and spiritually enrich the lives of everyone, regardless of their position in society.

This was why enlightened industrialists such as Titus Salt and Robert Owen thought it important to include schools, libraries, reading rooms and concert halls in their model villages alongside good quality housing and clean water. The aim was not social mobility, but dignity, greater happiness and personal fulfilment; for all their Victorian paternalism, they at least understood that the fruits of civilization are as cultural as they are practical.

It was not only rich industrialists that understood the inherent value of education. Many poorer people living during the industrial revolution understood that the benefits of education were inherent. Working-class intellectual groups, the flowering of self-improvement societies and the growth of the Sunday School movement all show that justifications of education were not always as instrumentalist as they are now (Griffin, 2014).

Indeed until quite recently there was a great tradition of working-class intellectualism. D.H. Lawrence, Alan Silitoe, the great pit village brass bands and even the Manic Street Preachers are all proof of the esteem in which many poorer communities once held learning and culture. Once again it is important to emphasise that this respect for knowledge and culture was not predicated on its capacity to materially advance those who learned it. These individuals and their communities understood that the real value was not in materially changing the world, but in the fact that it helped enrich individual experiences of it. Education probably would not change your position in society, but it might make you happier and more fulfilled.

This is a message that pupils in all our schools, especially the most supposedly disadvantaged, should hear. The reason they should work hard is not because exam results are a passport out of lives that 'high' or 'posh' society sneers at, but because what they learn gives them the ability to experience a richer existence while still remaining true to themselves. While it is not wrong to hope some of our pupils will be so captivated by what they learn that they wish to continue formally studying after they leave school, it would be unwise to make this the goal in itself, because by so doing we cast every pupil who does not as a failure.

At whole-school level, this makes curriculum more important than almost anything else.

If what is taught is not interesting, important and life-enriching then teachers will find it difficult to motivate pupils who, either rightly or wrongly, feel that passing exams is either impossible or pointless. For this reason, the quite recent increased attention placed on curriculum should be welcomed, and schools choosing to prioritise getting this right should be given time and help to do it. However, it would be naive to believe creating a great curriculum will in itself lead to greater pupil interest and motivation.

Creating and delivering a strong curriculum is tricky because unless content is carefully sequenced and incrementally built upon, a lack of requisite knowledge can make new, challenging topics so inaccessible they seem boring. Motivating pupils means making sure they hold the knowledge they need to unlock the next piece of content, which then becomes the knowledge they need to unlock the next piece, and so on.

Schools doing this are mistaken to talk much about public examination outcomes (especially before the latter stages of Year 11) as this implies to pupils that the main point of what they are learning is a specific grade, which means that those who feel they can't or think they won't achieve what their teachers hope for them are likely to switch off. Rather than saying to children that 'the reason you need to remember what you learn in Year 7 is so you'll get good grades', it is almost always better to say something along the lines of 'You need to remember what you learn in Year 7 so that you find Year 8 more interesting.' Happily, this message may lead to better outcomes as a side effect anyway, which may go some way to reassure school leaders still scarred by long years in which the dominant measure of school effectiveness was examination results.

Schools, particularly those in areas not traditionally academically aspirational, must actively create, cultivate and maintain cultures in which the pursuit and acquisition of knowledge is normalised. Those working in schools where this seems an impossible dream might take heart from the huge attitudinal changes that have taken place towards homophobia over the last few decades. Twenty years ago, 'gay' was an insult and homophobic comments in schools were relatively commonplace. The idea of a gay pupil or teacher being open about their sexuality would have seemed utterly absurd and in many contexts even masochistic. Although there remain lots of issues, in most schools things are much better now. While wider societal changes have driven this, schools have certainly played their part. Adopting policies which make it clear what is acceptable and what is not, educating pupils through lessons, assemblies and externally run programmes and having all adults aligned and united has contributed to a change about which we should all be proud. This change has not resulted in children feeling that by becoming less homophobic they have become less themselves.

Change does not have to be a zero-sum game. If schools successfully create cultures in which working hard and learning are regarded as components of a positive personal identity, then there is no reason young people should see the acquisition of knowledge as a betrayal of their core values.

To achieve this, schools must be clear and unashamed about their purpose. They are not community centres, babysitting services, police stations or youth clubs. Before anything else, they are academic institutions and everything they do should aim to promote learning.

Working hard must be normalised. Behaviour policies should go beyond focusing on visible examples of disruptive behaviour and create an expectation that children must be focused and work hard all the time. This is important because if passivity and inertia are permitted then some pupils will not learn enough to find what they study interesting. If this inertia then goes unchallenged, it will spread, making those pupils who do choose to work hard appear abnormal, which is powerful disincentive to diligence for children who (like everybody) want to feel as if they fit in.

Schools should also be thoughtful and careful about what they place in their curriculum and how they communicate these choices to pupils. Adjusting curriculum to make it 'relevant' (in the most reductive sense) or – still worse – 'accessible' to disadvantaged communities is at best short-termist and at worst counterproductive because it reinforces the view that 'difficult' so-called 'highbrow' culture is the preserve of elites, when the message we should be giving our children is that great work – from *Macbeth* to *I Know Why the Caged Bird Sings* – is the entitlement of everyone, regardless of their current station in life or where they will end up. Even if adjusting a curriculum to make it easier for pupils to achieve good exam results worked, the long-term opportunity cost of cutting children off from accessing trickier, more powerful and beautiful works in the future should be factored into decision making.

The goal should be that pupils leave school believing there are no aspects of culture which aren't open to them. Martin Robinson, author of *Trivium 21c*, calls this 'cultural mobility', which he describes really well here:

> Each subject helps make meaning for the child. This is the way this subject works, these are the finest thoughts, artefacts, methods and ideals that help us make sense of the world and, in turn, help the pupil to make their way through this world. (Robinson, 2019)

As tempting as it is to do so, teachers and leaders should be careful not to make too much of a fuss when communicating a challenging curriculum to disadvantaged pupils, because this implies that studying challenging work is unusual for pupils 'like them'. Instead of saying 'We're studying the *Odyssey* just like pupils at Eton do', it's probably better just to say 'We're studying the *Odyssey* because it's great!' The aim of school leaders – through curriculum, language, signage, assemblies and everything else – should be to create a sense of normalcy, which subtly but relentlessly builds, maintains and strengthens a community-wide belief that working hard to acquire academic knowledge is part and parcel of being a successful child, and that it is quite possible to do this without changing into something the child does not want to be.

Rather than shaking their fists at ivory towers, leaders and teachers should aim to build them in their schools.

Teachers working in contexts in which school cultures are at odds with this view will face more difficulties in motivating pupils to work but, nonetheless, there are still things they can do.

The first and perhaps most important of these is to demonstrate passion for the subjects they teach in a way that demonstrates they are not only means to an end. Instead of emphasising the importance of high grades (which is particularly hard work when talking to unmotivated pupils outside core subjects anyway), teachers should explain exactly why their disciplines are interesting for their own sake. This means keeping up to date with disciplinarily development and new scholarship, and sharing these with pupils. It means emphasising links and connections between different aspects of a curriculum and, wherever possible, avoiding sliding into the trap of trying to justify content through promising hypothetical extraneous rewards in some unimaginable future.

It is also important teachers make sure pupils have the opportunity to achieve regular success and understand what they need to do to improve in a meaningful, practical sense. This can be a particular problem for teachers in schools insisting on GCSE-style assessments from Year 7, making poor marks inevitable for many pupils – and there is very little as demoralising as continued failure. Where possible, teachers should avoid this and instead set stage- and age-appropriate assessments that allow children to achieve scores that show they are improving when they've worked hard. Teachers who must, through enforced policy, grade their pupils using GCSE mark schemes may be able to mitigate some of the disheartening effects by setting pupils regular, low-stakes quizzes in which improvement is more realistic and clearer. Pupils are also likely to benefit from tight, specific goal-setting which is focused on discrete areas of knowledge rather than vague, generic targets that are hard to understand and even harder to act upon. For example, setting a goal like 'Go back over the reasons for William's invasion of England in 1066 and learn them for a test next week' is much clearer than the general advice to 'include a range of causes when explaining the reasons for events'.

Doing this with younger pupils who have not yet decided school isn't relevant to them is obviously easier than it is with older pupils who've already mentally checked out and know it won't be long before they leave. That said, in some cases it is possible to motivate even those just weeks away from final exams. Although they are good at hiding it, many pupils do fear their final exams because they know they won't do well. These young people are very unlikely to respond positively to questions like 'Don't you want to pass?', or 'If you work really hard, you can get a grade 9!', because they are sure neither is possible. Instead, it is best to simply focus on the specifics of what they need to do in order to get better from their own starting point. This is why target grades – still used by many, many schools – can be very unhelpful (Newmark, 2017). Telling a pupil with a target grade of a 9, but who is actually only achieving 2s, that they 'need to work hard to get your target grade' is at best just plain ridiculous and at worse completely demoralising, as it implies that even if there is improvement, any grade below their target represents just a different degree of failure. Teachers have a better chance of getting these pupils to work hard if they give instructions like 'You need to learn the information on page 32 of your revision guide using the "read, cover, write" method and then answer these questions without using your notes.'

However hard they work, not all teachers will be successful in motivating all their pupils. They should not become disheartened. Those who feel they are making no progress at all should remember that, in many circumstances, the odds are against them, but that this doesn't make what they are trying to do any less worthwhile. Education itself is a moral act and neither success nor failure changes that. When we fulfil our duty by teaching as well as we can, we are entitled to feel proud of ourselves, however our pupils respond.

Why is teaching making me so sick?

I've been a teacher for two years now. Since starting, I've put on a stone and a half, stopped all exercise in term time and am eating far too much junk food. I'm also worried that I'm drinking too much. I feel sluggish all the time and sometimes get out of breath just walking between classrooms. I don't sleep well and often feel anxious. Every term I seem to get ill and struggle on until the holidays – when I collapse. Some weekend days I can barely bring myself to go out of the house. I've invested a lot in teaching and don't want to give it up, but I am worried about my physical and mental health.

This problem can't be addressed without acknowledging the impact of very long hours. Overwork does lead to stress and poor health and teachers who are made to do too much, or choose to do more than they need to, are of course more prone to problems.

Long hours spent doing work cut into time that could be spent doing things that contribute to good health. Anyone starting work at seven in the morning and working through to seven in the evening, or later, will struggle to find time to cook proper meals. Eating high-fat ready meals or takeaways, snacking on sugar and finding bursts of energy in caffeine can quickly create a pattern of peaks and troughs that is hard to break. Even if people working this long can summon the willpower to exercise, it is likely they'll find workouts comparatively unsatisfying, which affects motivation in the longer term. All this damages quality sleep, which means the high-sugar, high-fat and high-caffeine diets feel necessary in order to push through the day. For teachers in this situation, alcohol (or indeed any other addictive substance) can be very tempting because it provides a shortcut to altered consciousness, which gives the illusion of switching off. For most people, though, drinking immoderately takes far more than it gives and contributes to the issues that started problems in the first place.

All that said, the truth is certainly more subtle than 'long hours cause bad health'. Plenty of people in all sorts of jobs, including teaching, work very long hours and thrive. Some people who work comparatively few hours suffer from lifestyle health problems, too, which means things must be more complicated.

To understand why some thrive and some don't, whatever context they are in, it might be helpful to begin by considering what it is that makes some people quite able to cope with a large volume of work and the long hours required to complete it. First, it is important to recognise that people who feel they are being successful and making progress at things they care about are typically far happier with high workloads than those who feel they are failing at things they don't think important. When things are going well and we can see a direct benefit of what we're doing, we don't mind working very hard and may even find ourselves energised. While we may know our hours are excessive, and be mindful of the impact this is having on those close to us, we are less likely to find the time spent working stressful in itself. Teachers perceived to be doing a good job working in high-performing schools with autonomy to plan, teach and assess in the ways they think best are probably less likely to find long hours stressful, because there is a pay off to self-esteem, career prospects and perhaps even their own finances.

Teachers working in less happy contexts are far more likely to suffer mentally and physically. For those under the cosh, whether it is because of questions around their own competence or concerns about the perceived quality of the schools in which they work, perpetual anxiety can quickly make long hours feel unbearable. In an unfortunate double-whammy, teachers working in environments like this are those least likely to be given professional freedom, which makes work feel even more like drudgery. If results do not improve, which they may well not given the limited influence teachers have, all tasks come to feel pointless, which can quickly create a demotivating sense of futility and senselessness. The frustrations of working like this for hours and hours, day in and day out, can very quickly spill into other areas of life: even if you have the time, it's hard to find the energy to go for a run or cook a proper meal from scratch when you've spent your day in a state of low-level panic about the length of your to-do list. It is far easier to drink half a bottle of wine, eat a pizza and try to forget you're likely to wake at 4 a.m. saucer-eyed and too nauseous to eat anything before the breaktime doughnut you haven't the willpower to resist.

Unfortunately some schools do buy into the inevitability of this, whether consciously or unconsciously, by creating cultures that endorse and even validate it. In some schools, heads begin the countdown to the next holiday on the first day back after the last one. This, while superficially a positive example of in-it-together camaraderie ('Just 27 get-ups until Christmas, guys!'), actually sends a negative message because it is an admission that the coming term will be relentlessly brutal, and that the best way to get through is to remind yourself that at some point in the future it will end. This feast-and-famine approach to life makes developing consistent, healthy patterns really difficult. Motivating yourself to exercise or eat better for seven days after six weeks of inactivity and sugar can be so hard it doesn't feel worth bothering, especially as those who do make changes are unlikely to see any benefits in such a short space of time.

Some schools go further by normalising the binge-eating of biscuits, cake, confectionery and sweets during term time. The stressful, pressurised nature of the job can mean it is conveniently assumed that eating poorly is simply unavoidable and providing sugary treats is seen as a duty of those chairing meetings. Those choosing not to tuck in can find themselves, good naturedly but persuasively, pressured into having 'just a slice'. While saying there is never a place for such indulgences would be going too far, it is important to accept that it is harder to stay healthy if snacking is made a regular feature of day-to-day professional interaction.

Some teachers, concerned about relative inactivity and poor nutrition, fall victim to the myth that teaching is such a physically demanding profession in itself that it compensates for a lack of purposeful exercise and a problematic diet. This, on the face of it, is not a stupid thing to believe. Teaching is, of course, more active than many jobs, particularly those based predominantly in offices. Typical teachers do move a fair amount and even the act of standing in front of a class and explaining something burns more calories than working on a computer. Unfortunately though, making a simple comparison like this is flawed.

Firstly, work for most teachers is not as active as many believe it to be. Those who teach in one classroom and move no further than the staffroom are unlikely to be burning very many more calories than someone working in an office. Of course, PE teachers and those with responsibilities that take them over a large school site will expend more energy; but unless they are getting out of breath fairly regularly, even these are probably not exercising as much as they should.

Secondly, those with more sedentary jobs at all concerned about their health are likely to be aware they aren't getting enough exercise and so, sometimes literally, take steps to compensate. Increasingly, flexible working arrangements mean office-based workers make time in their day, even at lunch, to do some form of physical activity. In schools, such flexibility is rare. This, added to punishingly long hours which make working through break and lunch common, makes it much harder for teachers to do the same.

Many schools do recognise the unhealthy lifestyles of their staff as an issue and run well-meaning initiatives (typically called things like 'Healthy Schools') to address it. These usually involve a focus on better eating and may include stress-busting programmes like mindfulness, sports clubs for staff and yoga. While the thinking is admirable, such policies can never have more than a limited impact if they deal only with the symptoms of poor health while ignoring the causes. It is all very well offering beautician appointments in non-contact time, or a running club at 3.30, but if workloads are too high for people to spare the time to attend them then they will not be beneficial to most teachers. Indeed, it is even possible they can make things worse because they can lead school staff at all levels to feel poor lifestyles are actually the fault of individuals for not taking advantage of school provision, which means less focus on changing negative aspects of the overall environment itself.

Some things, admittedly, schools can do very little about. Teachers are more prone to illness than those in many other professions because the nature of their work exposes them to more germs. Schools are full of people, both children and adults, and can act as vectors for coughs, colds, flu and stomach bugs. There is a fairly direct link between standing in front of a class of spluttering children and becoming poorly yourself. That children as a whole are not a demographic typified by high standard of personal hygiene makes the situation worse and means those who work in schools are more likely to get an illness than those working in offices. It probably isn't fair to pin all the blame for this on students though; very busy, time-pressured working environments make us all, at times, less fastidious about things like hand-washing and dirty tissues than we know we should be. Remembering this can help us avoid falling for the narrative that our various ailments are inevitably caused by stress and unhealthy lifestyles. While of course these do play a role in lowering immune systems, they alone are not the cause of the end-of-term flu.

Finally, it is again worth examining the harmful but pervasive belief that good teachers are always busy and stressed. This is silliness and easily leads schools and teachers to the conclusion that unbalanced, unhealthy lifestyles are unavoidable and there is no place in the profession for those who are either unable or unwilling to accept them. Teachers simply must reject such thinking. Those that do not, victims of a sort of Stockholm syndrome, are contributors to the sort of culture in which bad health can seem an occupational hazard and becomes normalised, so hiding the true extent of the problem.

What to do

Anyone who has ever been on an aeroplane knows that the pre-flight safety briefing says they should put on their own air mask before helping a child. This is always quite jarring to hear. Our instincts tell us that when it counts our first responsibility is to those we care most about, not ourselves. To understand why we get this advice it is important to remember that the airline is not making a judgement about whose life is more valuable. It is a recognition that if, due to a lack of oxygen (or whatever reason), an adult becomes incapacitated, then they are no longer in a position to provide help to anyone at all.

There are lessons in this for those in danger of burning themselves out. When we are not healthy, we do everything worse. Detailed planning may well be done but it is likely to be poor. Teaching when exhausted is a recipe for disaster. Marking and assessing may fulfil all the requirements of a policy but are far less likely to address the most pertinent areas. Even teachers who are able to compartmentalise so well that their pupils don't notice a difference are very unlikely to be able to keep it up forever. Teachers who leave the profession because their health becomes so poor deprive future generations of pupils of an experienced, competent practitioner, which means even an apparent short-term victory can result in a far-reaching and more important defeat.

To be fair on ourselves and our pupils, we must begin by accepting that our first priority must be our own health and wellbeing. Only when this is assured can we properly prioritise the needs of those we are responsible for.

Of course, this is much easier said than done.

Exercise is a good place to start because, done regularly, it can provide a structure on which to hang other things. While meaningfully training for a marathon might be unrealistic for many teachers, especially who those who feel they often don't have time to go to the toilet, even a very small amount of exercise can improve wellbeing. Committing to a brisk 20-minute walk three times a week, preferably at set times, and sticking to it come hell, highwater or Ofsted can be a really positive step towards restoring balance because it makes physical activity a feature of a properly structured week. It also makes increasing volume and intensity of exercise later easier: going from nothing to hard workouts feels like an intimidatingly huge step whereas establishing even a very low level of basic fitness makes a small increase feel more achievable.

Those willing and able to push themselves a bit harder are likely to get more benefits. Being out of breath and sweaty can have a meditative effect because it focuses attention. It is actually quite difficult to be anxious about an impending lesson observation or deadline when your mind is set on getting up a hill without stopping or bench-pressing a weight right at the top end of your capability. While the effect is of course only temporary, there are longer-term benefits to clearing your mind completely a few times a week because it provides a sense of perspective that may make it easier to switch off at other times. Finally, when work is at its worst and it feels like we're making no progress at all, improving at something else – whether getting faster, stronger or just generally fitter – can give a greater sense of control and help reinforce self-esteem, which has a beneficial knock-on effect. While for most people, exercise has perhaps the greatest overall benefit, it is also worth noting that other hobbies can help too. Playing a musical instrument or painting a picture won't reduce weight or make those doing them fitter, but the act of purposeful attention on something other than work has benefits too.

Another benefit of physical activity is that it can provide more motivation to eat better because it makes the effects of not doing so much more obvious. While eating badly is even more damaging without exercise, the impact of it often isn't immediately clear because those who aren't pushing themselves are far less likely to notice until they're in a really bad state. It is generally easier to resist wall-to-wall cake or three beers in the evening if you know that regularly indulging will mean you're less able to run your twice-weekly 5K without stopping for a rest halfway through. Once again it is worth emphasising the importance of following through on a commitment to exercise because otherwise good intentions can act as an excuse for not making changes to diet. It is all too easy to succumb to the biscuit tin by thinking 'I'll burn this off in the holidays', and then finding other reasons not to exercise when they finally arrive.

Those who find themselves unable to exercise at all (or do much less than they are used to) will have to make changes to their eating habits if they don't want to put on weight. What works is very individual so it would probably be a mistake to go into this in too much detail beyond some basic well-established rules: eat three meals and don't skip breakfast; watch portion size; and make sure that calorie intake does not exceed what's burnt. Some teachers find it helpful to bring everything they eat into school, including snacks, which makes substitutions easier. While it is always difficult to resist cake when everyone else is eating it, it's easier if you have chunks of pineapple or even just an apple to eat instead. It's also worth remembering that what seems a craving for alcohol is often actually hunger, which means that eating sensibly and regularly can lead to a reduction in high-calorie wine, beer or spirits in the evening.

An empty fridge makes stopping at a takeaway or a rushed trip to the supermarket for a ready meal tempting. Planning meals on Saturday or Sunday can help teachers avoid their good intentions evaporating the following week, as well as helping save money. For those teachers who have time to do it, batch-cooking meals can be even more helpful because heating these up can actually take less time and be less hassle than ordering a takeaway. For those who struggle to do this, but do cook sometimes, simply making double or more of the amount you usually eat and freezing the rest can be just as easy.

Before finishing up on diet, it is important to acknowledge that a few teachers find losing too much weight more of a problem. Those who find this happening to them must, of course, take action too. These people simply have to make sure they eat healthily and regularly to avoid further problems.

A lot of teachers who take steps to increase exercise and eat properly will find they sleep better without doing anything else at all. Establishing a set of patterns and routines creates a reassuring sense of order and regularity that makes falling and staying asleep less of a struggle. However, even those who adopt a sensible, balanced lifestyle can still experience problems.

Tolerating less sleep in the week and trying to compensate with lie-ins at the weekend is usually a mistake. Firstly, this doesn't really work because it makes establishing regularity impossible. Those that sleep in late on Saturday and Sunday are likely to find it difficult to get to sleep early on Sunday night, which means they won't have had enough rest when the alarm rings on Monday. This deficit can make caffeine and sugar feel necessary to stay alert throughout the day, making it more difficult to drop off at an appropriate time. Many teachers don't actually recognise this as a problem because they are working late into the evenings anyway but this pattern, of course, creates further issues. While it does require some discipline to do it (especially for those who enjoy late nights at the weekend), getting up and going to bed at the same time each day is more sensible for most people.

Those that do work right up to bedtime typically find it harder to get drowsy and then fall asleep because they are likely to still be thinking about the things they were working on. This is even tougher for those anxious about how this work will be judged, which is another reason to be wary of schools with extensive and punitive quality-assurance measures. Teachers, like everyone else, should make time to unwind and relax before trying to go to sleep. To avoid sitting around and worrying, which is no more productive than just doing the work, it is important to do something else and to fully focus on it. Playing a musical instrument, having a conversation about something other than teaching, drawing, reading a novel or even doing something as simple as properly watching a film or TV programme works – so long as attention is fully on this activity. At all costs, avoid trying to do any of these things at the same time as working because that isn't unwinding at all. Anything done like this will be of lower quality and will take longer anyway, negating any of the perceived benefits. It should go without saying that email and social media are also considerable dangers, especially if messages and notifications are school related; it's very hard to not think about school when your phone is constantly reminding you of it. If you can get away with it, don't have work email on your phone and switch it off, or at least on silent in another room, when preparing to sleep.

Drinking less alcohol also has benefits to sleep. While the effects of alcohol can, superficially at least, soothe anxiety and help some people feel calmer, this is usually only temporary. Not drinking at all, at least in the week, is probably a good idea – but any reduction will have some benefits. If stopping altogether feels unrealistic, switching to lower-unit drinks, which are increasingly easy to find, can be beneficial to those too habituated to cease indulging altogether.

The changes described so far are likely to make it easier to fall asleep in the first place, but some unlucky teachers will still find they wake in the middle of the night, sometimes for hours at a time. This is truly miserable; turning over and switching on a light to see the clock says three or four in the morning can be so depressing, especially when it happens regularly. This is far more common for those feeling generally anxious. If this happens, tossing and turning in bed is usually not the answer; but nor is getting up and doing work – or, as I have done before, even going in to school only to find it dark and locked up. It is better to leave the bedroom and do something intellectually undemanding for half an hour or so before trying again. In the midst of all this, it can also be helpful to try to retain perspective; in the small hours, insomnia can be anxiety inducing in itself, with the prospect of the day ahead, already demanding, seeming truly horrific. If this happens to you, remind yourself that fatigue is not, in itself, life threatening. Like driving (for most of us), many of the processes of teaching are automated, and while it is of course unpleasant to do so, most of us are able to get through a working day on very little sleep. That said, it is a serious problem and those experiencing insomnia regularly should get professional help.

It would not be honest to finish this chapter without acknowledging that, as with almost everything in teaching, context is of huge importance. Some schools do make living a healthy lifestyle impossible and teachers working in these should feel no guilt in moving on to more enlightened institutions. Once again, it is worth remembering that careers should be long – marathons, not sprints. While martyring yourself can seem noble if – as is very likely – this results in a departure from teaching altogether, the overall (potentially multi-decade) cost is much, much too high.

Looking after yourself does not make you weak. It marks you out as a true professional.

Why teach?

In England it feels as if we are finding this question harder and harder to answer.

Year on year, we fail to hit teacher training recruitment targets and lose more and more teachers to private family lives and other professions.

As the number of children in our schools rises, alarm is turning into panic.

There are, of course, many reasons for this. The familiar culprits of poor behaviour, crude accountability measures, falling wages and inflexible working conditions have probably all played a part.

But there are more fundamental, existential questions to answer too. This chapter will outline four common consequentialist justifications for teaching as a profession, explore their flaws and limitations, then aim to explain why, irrespective of all these, teaching is still profoundly moral and worthwhile.

Do teachers make society more equal?

Fifteen years ago, part of the way in which I was drawn into teaching was a lie.

I was told (and believed) that because teachers were directly responsible for the grades their pupils got in public examinations, good teachers working in poor areas were helping redress societal inequality. The argument went that better teaching in poorer areas led to better grades for poorer children, which led to them going to better universities, which meant they got better jobs and then earned more money. The outcome of my work would be that poorer children became richer adults. Gradually but inexorably, I was helping construct a true meritocracy.

This argument, which is particularly attractive to the young who want to change the world, has not gone away.

Well-meaning teacher training programmes, particularly those working in areas of disadvantage, still use the gap between the richer and poorer sections of society as a way of signing up new recruits. We see this in adverts in which poor pupils talk enthusiastically about the impact a teacher made in setting them on the way to high-flying, influential careers; and we see it when England's Department of Education proudly crows the narrowing of attainment gaps between poorer and richer children.

Such messages are compelling. Most of us want to feel our lives have mattered. Righting the wrongs of life's injustices seems a noble way to live and find meaning.

The problem here is that, while there will always be examples that stand out as exceptions, we have little evidence that the gap between rich and poor people in Britain has narrowed or will narrow in the future. Much evidence suggests the opposite: that the gap is widening (Chu, 2017). If we accept this but persist in believing that the main reason for public education and teaching is to narrow differences in wealth, then we must accept that we have failed in the past, are failing now, and in all likelihood will continue to fail in the future. Recent surveys suggest that our younger generations are quite aware of this and are increasingly cynical (or actually realistic?) about the idea of social mobility (Weale, 2018).

This should not come as much of a shock given the nature of our mostly cohort-referenced public examination system, which effectively caps the number of top grades that can be achieved each year based on attainment in tests taken at age ten or eleven. Everyone involved in the care of a child – and of course the child themselves – is incentivised to use every advantage they have to outcompete other children of the same age. Those with more advantage will usually outcompete those with less, and so go on to more prestigious university courses and better-paid careers. If the whole cohort improves, then those in a position to do so will make sure the children they care about will improve more than others. Once again, it is the most advantaged who are in the best position to do this. While it might be a stretch to say things have been set up this way deliberately, the effect is the same: divisions in educational attainment are maintained or even widened.

Cohort referencing means we are being dishonest when we say to all our pupils 'Work hard and you will get a good grade', because the limited allocation of each grade means that this is not true for everyone. Those blessed with advantage – be it affluence or higher intelligence – are always likely to do better than those less fortunate. The worst consequence of all this might be that by tying the value of what we teach to a test score, we imply that those who do not get a high grade have been wasting their time. This is particularly alarming when we remind ourselves that the whole way examinations are set up makes it simply impossible for all pupils to reach the top of the ladder.

For some pupils to do better, others have to do worse.

The playing field is not level. If we teach to reduce social inequality then we are failures.

Further evidence of this can be seen in admission figures to the best universities, which show that while more pupils overall are going on to university, there has been little if any improvement in the proportion of poorer young people going to Oxbridge and Russell Group institutions. This is important. While the number of highly paid, prestigious jobs remains the same (and may even decline if our economy contracts after Brexit), it would be entirely illogical to assume that the act of going to university, particularly if it is less prestigious, will lead to greater affluence (Garner, 2016).

Perhaps we could treat the justification of education as driving social mobility more seriously if those that made it had plans to make richer pupils perform worse in order to make space at life's top table. This, of course and quite rightly for all sorts of reasons, will never happen. No sane government would ever introduce a law making it illegal for parents to pay for private tuition for their child, or banning them from reading to their children before bedtime to help them with literacy.

Do teachers make society happier?

Even if we accept that our work does not narrow divisions, it might still be possible to form an argument that it is a consequentially justified activity if we could prove that society in its entirety was becoming more educated and happier as a result of our collective work.

Intellectually, at least, this argument does carry some weight. Educated societies do, on the whole, seem to be more peaceful, tolerant and prosperous. It is not a huge stretch to extend this to the belief that should we improve the overall level of education (effectively shoving the bell curve right) – then, the work of teachers would, overall, lead to the general betterment of society even if the divisions within it remain as acute as ever. This is a version of a classic capitalist argument in its belief that competition between individuals and groups results in an overall improvement from which everyone eventually benefits, even if inequalities are never ironed out.

To decide whether or not this is a legitimate reason to teach, we need to look at whether England is actually becoming more educated over time, then work out if this is because of schools, before considering whether or not any rise has increased general happiness.

David Didau, who tweets @DavidDidau, has done work on this. In a sequence of blog posts and in his new book, he has demonstrated that if we take IQ as a measure of intelligence (and I do realise this is disputed), then our children, as a whole, do seem to be getting cleverer.

The problem here is that it isn't clear whether this has been the result of schooling. This may seem counterintuitive, given the stated aim of schools; but it is important to remember that children actually spend a very small proportion of their lives in lessons. IQ tests assess ability to think in the abstract, and it is just as likely that rises in scores are attributable to an increasingly complicated world that requires its inhabitants to think in an abstract fashion. This seems to be borne out by bigger increases in IQ scores in developing countries which are undergoing very rapid technological and industrial changes than in developed societies which went through these changes longer ago (Didau, 2017b). While David Didau has good reason to disagree with this, citing research which tracked differences in increases in IQ between pupils of different ages in the same year, I still don't think there's enough evidence for us to say with absolute confidence that England is becoming any better educated as a result of the work of its teachers. Although there is evidence that IQ has risen over recent years, and schools probably have contributed to this, the many societal changes that have happened in the same period mean we cannot be sure that this has been only – or perhaps even mainly – the result of the work of schools. What's more, depressingly and alarmingly, it appears that literacy and numeracy rates may now actually be declining. We are the only OECD country in which literacy levels of people aged between 16 and 24 are lower than those of people aged 55 and over, which suggests our society may actually be becoming *less* rather than *more* educated (Ramesh, 2013).

It is at least possible that our recent preoccupation with examination outcomes as proxies of education may well have worsened the overall quality of education in England. Brutal, unsophisticated and high-stakes accountability incentivised schools to game-play with low-value qualifications and to teach to tests. What may have worked for individual schools may well have failed the collective if the overall aim was a better-educated society. Encouragingly, it does seem that Ofsted, England's school inspectorate, is acknowledging this as a risk with its latest framework; but it is far too early to tell how successful they are likely to be.

Even if we put all this aside and could prove not only that our children are getting cleverer but that they will continue to become cleverer and that this is because of our schools, it would still be impossible to say whether this has benefited society. This is because we can't say whether people in the past were any happier than we are today. While we can make judgements based upon our own values, the inherent bias in making such judgements invalidates them. We may look at the life of a medieval peasant and shudder at the thought of their pain and suffering, but our shudders are because we are imagining *ourselves* as *them*. What we fail to get is that if we were *them*, we wouldn't be *us*. We don't know what it was like to be illiterate in a culture in which nearly everyone was illiterate. We don't know what it was like to have a certainty of faith that meant we knew our souls would still exist for eternity after death. This is not to say that men and women in the past were happier than us, but it does mean we simply can't make an accurate assessment as to whether or not being better educated, however we define this, leads to greater happiness.

It would be unfair to move on before acknowledging the correlation between higher IQs and greater happiness in individuals, and how this might lead some teachers to argue that teaching can still be consequentially justified if the result of a teacher's work is cleverer (and therefore happier) children. The problem here is that it is not clear that higher intelligence in itself is the cause of greater happiness, even if those with higher intelligence do tend to be happier. Life is largely a zero-sum game, with greater opportunities afforded to those who win. It is entirely possible, even likely, that it is greater opportunities which are the source of any greater happiness, not intelligence in of itself. This means that even if teaching did make children cleverer, unless this resulted in greater opportunity (which is something entirely different), then it is unlikely that people as a whole will end up any more content than they are now. Finally, it is worth thinking about how happy so-called child geniuses end up – the picture is, at best, very mixed.

So no. The argument that teaching leads to a more educated and therefore happier society is not robust enough to use as a justification for why teachers do what they do.

Do teachers make society better?

Some teachers believe the most important purpose of education is to make our world a morally better place. The argument goes that the world is unfair and that this unfairness is the result of flaws in the people who have constructed the societies in which they live. Children in school offer us a fresh start. If we can teach them to be less prejudiced, more honest and selfless, then the world they create when they grow up will be better than the world we live in now.

This justification for education seems heavily influenced by philosophers who argued humans were born good and were made wicked by negative outside influence. If we could eliminate negative influences then humans will not behave badly and the world will be better for everyone.

Alternatively, others claim that children are naturally selfish and will behave badly without corrective influences. They may argue that it is possible to create a better society by rewarding pupils for good behaviour and punishing them for bad. If we do this well then children will eventually internalise good values, which will lead to a better society.

There are lots of problems with both these approaches.

The first of these is how we define what a 'better' society looks like. There is no consensus. For some people this might mean the withering away of the state and the final realisation of Marx's communist dream; for others it may mean an orderly, traditional societal structure in which rigid hierarchies provide stability and security. If we cannot agree on the ideal society then it is impossible for us ever to achieve a result that satisfies everyone. One person's dream is another's dystopian nightmare. Those who do not understand this are either naive or dangerous ideologues – or both. Teaching in a way designed to create a specific type of society means teaching children that those with alternative views are either misguided or wicked, which encourages narrow thinking and intolerance.

Even if we could all agree on what kind of society we want to create, there's little reason to think schools could deliver it. In a typical year, most children spend less than 10% of their time in front of their teachers, meaning most of the time they are exposed to influences beyond the reach of their schools. This means that any child's views are likely to be influenced far more by their parents, friends and those they admire than they are the work of their teachers. While some countries, including Nazi Germany in the past and North Korea today, have tried hard to drastically increase the influence of schools to create the sort of society they deem desirable, most of us would not feel comfortable emulating their methods.

Do teachers make people more productive?

Every day in England, pupils interrupt their lessons to ask 'Why do we need to learn this?' What often follows is teachers parroting learned consequentialist justifications. In my subject, history, this might be a teacher saying 'If you understand that people in the past had different views, then you'll understand that people today have too. And this will mean you get on with people better when you get a job.' But trying to justify the content of our curriculum by its capacity for practical application is flawed. Beyond basic literacy and numeracy, most of what is learned in school is not obviously useful in the wider world without making absurd leaps. This is something many of the pupils I have taught have been acutely aware of. (It can nevertheless be amusing to try to construct contrived situations that justify the teaching of something pupils regard as obscure – for example, 'If you become a baker and your till breaks and you have to work out how much Mrs Jones owes you and nobody has a calculator or a phone and there's no way you'll be able to get one then this algebra is going to come in really handy!')

Still worse, if we allow pupils to make this argument, we are suggesting that the only subjects which are important are those with a clear and direct link to practical tasks pupils might do in the future. While some might argue this is actually quite right, curriculums developed on this principle would be radically different to most of those we deliver in schools today. Out with Homer and the irrelevant Renaissance artists! In with using Excel and developing a good phone voice!

Do we really want our young people to learn only what is practically useful?

It is clear to me that no consequentialist argument is strong enough to work as a justification for educating our children. As much as we might want to, we cannot say 'We teach children in schools so that X will happen' because we can't agree what we want; we can't prove that anything we want to happen does actually happen; and even if we could all agree that a change that had happened was a positive one, it would be impossible to prove that this change was the result of the work of teachers.

For many of us, accepting this means facing something of an existential crisis. If nothing good comes of our work then why bother doing it at all?

This story might be a helpful way of concentrating the argument.

Not very long ago, I heard about a senior leader who had a meeting with a teaching assistant assigned to work with a pupil suffering from a progressive disease which meant he used a wheelchair and was not expected to live beyond his early twenties. The meeting was called because there were concerns the pupil wasn't getting proper support, with the TA often appearing to be uninterested and bored. In the meeting, the assistant accepted she had not been effectively supporting the young person and told the leader that she would prefer to prepare small groups of gifted pupils for Oxford and Cambridge University. When the senior leader asked them why they didn't want to work with the disabled pupil they'd been directed to help, they were horrified to hear the reply: 'It's not like there's any point. It's not like he's ever going to do anything.'

Upsetting, no? But if we derive our sense of purpose as teachers from consequentialism, then what right do we have to be upset?? Whatever grades the young man got, he almost certainly would not go to university. He was even less likely to ever have a job. His early death would mean that, in the big scheme of things, how well educated he ends up is irrelevant to the general education level of society. Lastly, he would play no part in future society because he would not be part of it. So what does it matter whether or not school equips him with the personal qualities or skills needed to impact on the world?

If we accept consequentialism then there is no point in educating young people like him at all, which makes the teaching assistant right.

What nonsense. She was wrong and we know it.

The story makes us uneasy because on a deeper, instinctive level, we know that the value of education is not in any outcomes we hope will be a result of it.

Instead, the true value of education is in the inherent worth of what pupils learn and their entitlement to it regardless of anything that might or might not happen to them in the future.

While justifying education in this way may feel unfamiliar, it is not actually new at all. Our obsession with consequentialism may actually be quite recent. For hundreds of years, an important reason for education was that what was taught was believed to have great inherent value. Everything taught was a precious jewel to be passed down through the generations. This has perhaps been most famously expressed by poet and inspector of schools Matthew Arnold, who wrote in 1869 that the purpose of education should be for young people to know 'the best that has been thought and said'. Those tempted to dismiss this as the privileged witterings of a Victorian man with a Messiah complex may be interested to learn that precisely the same sentiment was expressed by Arnold's socialist contemporary Robert Tressell in *The Ragged-Trousered Philanthropists*:

> What we call civilisation – the accumulation of knowledge which has come to us from our forefathers – is the fruit of thousands of years of human thought and toil ... It is by right the common heritage of all. Every little child that is born into the world, no matter whether he is clever or dull, whether he is physically perfect or lame, or blind; no matter how much he may excel or fall short of his fellows in other respects, in one thing at least he is their equal – he is one of the heirs of all the ages that have gone before. (Tressell, 2012)

This offers us a way forward.

In recognising that the point of what we do lies in the inherent value of what we teach our children, and letting go of the idea that we need something else to happen as a result of it, we can find real and robust purpose.

We cannot shake consequentialism completely. If we are to establish the bestowal of knowledge as teaching's raison d'etre, we have to believe that the children we are responsible for will recognise the value of what they learn. While this is of course still consequentialist, it is much less of a stretch than the belief that studying *Hamlet* will result in a measurable outcome in a completely different domain. It is far more realistic for a teacher to say 'I hope that by learning Hamlet's soliloquy pupils will see that people often struggle with feelings of pointlessness' than it is for them to say we teach Shakespeare because it will make our pupils richer. We can have even more confidence in pupils recognising the inherent value of 'the best that has been thought and said' if what we teach has been recognised as being of great worth by many people over a long period of time. This is why teaching children the *Odyssey* is better than teaching them *Harry Potter* or *Holes*. It is why we do pupils a disservice if we teach them the history of football instead of the *Magna Carta*. It is why a geography teacher is right to focus on glaciation and wrong to allow their pupils to spend valuable lesson time colouring in and labelling blank maps.

I think we should push past Arnold's narrow view of what is considered academic in the strictest sense too, expanding 'the best that has been thought and said' to include the best that has been made, cooked, danced and so on. Deciding whether pupils will learn to cook a rogan josh or a chicken tikka masala, or learn whether a dovetail joint is a better use of time than a mortise and tenon, should be just as important as deciding whether or not pupils should learn about the Napoleonic wars. There will never be agreement, but the most important debates we have in schools should be over what exactly we should teach our children based on intrinsic and inherent worth. On a subject of such importance, there will never be agreement; but these are the conversations we should be having. We should be arguing about whether we should include Aphra Behn's *Oroonoko* on our curriculum. We should be arguing about exactly which gothic novel should be taught.

Schools should not adapt what pupils learn based on what we think they will become. Instead they should teach children to alter themselves in order to become part of something greater. We all have voices but we sing as part of a choir. Our curriculum should whisper to our children 'You belong. You did not come from nowhere. All this came before you.'

This, the antithesis to the way in which child-centred education has been understood and interpreted in many English schools in recent years, may not sit comfortably with those who feel that teachers should make changes in response to whoever they find in front of them. Those feeling uneasy might want to think about how transformative and liberating it is to utterly lose yourself in a mathematical equation, poem, painting or piece of music. Curriculum is a powerful alchemy which can take a person out of their own limited experience and connect them to something so much larger. This is the real treasure. To allow our pupils to experience this, we must first help them shake off the intrusive egos that push all of us into imposing ourselves on whatever we encounter, whether in school or elsewhere.

This idea was developed in Simone Weil's 1942 essay 'Reflections on the Right Use of School Studies with a View to the Love of God' (Weil, 2012), which expresses the view that the primary purpose of schools should be to teach pupils to pay proper attention to what they are taught. While she sees the ultimate aim to be an increase in the capacity for prayer, we do not need to go this far to see better attention as a worthwhile end. If we teach pupils to see the value in subsuming their own egos and individual characteristics into what they are learning and free them from the oppressive belief that what they do in their classrooms is only worth the bother if they are materially rewarded for it, we create an inclusive sense of meaning achievable for everyone.

This provides schools and the teachers in them with a powerful sense of purpose that enables us to throw off the existential horror in realising that we cannot be sure anything we do ever leads to anything else. It also presents us with a great, grave responsibility. If none of our actions lead to the outcomes we once thought they did, and the only value of what we teach is in the intrinsic worth of the material itself, then what and how well we teach assumes immeasurable significance.

In this we are saved. We do not teach because by doing so we can eradicate the differences between rich and poor. We do not teach to educate society, or to create a better social system.. We do not educate our children so that they have 'skills' that will lead to them being more productive workers. Our responsibility is more profound. We teach because, as Tressell has said, our children are the heirs of all that has gone before them, and by teaching them well we gift them their birth right to the fruit of our civilizations.

How important, then, is what we teach and how well we do it? There is so much to learn and so little, little time. When we make decisions about curriculum, we do so as part of a great, great tradition. For hundreds of years, societies have been taking the baton of knowledge and passing it down through their generations and, by doing so, showing their children that they are valued, important and part of something so much more enormous than they are.

So if you are a teacher and you, now or in years to come, find yourself doubting whether what you do has real purpose, get up early and stand in any settlement in England. Watch the buses, silly uniforms and clip-on ties go by. Smile at the important, ritualistic frivolity. Think of the schools that breathe in our children in the morning and exhale them in the afternoon. Think about how little these children knew when they started school, and how much they know now, and how much they will know in the future. Think about how barren their lives would be if there were no schools or teachers and they were never taught anything at all. Think about how poor they would be in the most important sense if there were no schools and no teachers.

Think about this and allow yourself to feel the privilege and enormous weight of responsibility you carry, a weight that goes back hundreds of thousands of years. Picture yourself as a link in the only chain that really matters, a runner with a flaming torch you are thrusting into the hands of younger athletes so it won't matter that one day, sooner than anyone ever thinks they will, your legs will fail. Remember that even if one of your young athletes does fall, they had the same right to run as their luckier compatriots.

Remember we are all part of race in which the aim is not to win but to just keep going.

We are the links in the chain.

We are the runners in the race.

We are the bearers of the torch.

And this is why we teach.

'Academic work is one of those fields which contain a pearl so precious that it is worthwhile to sell all our possessions, keeping nothing for ourselves, in order to be able to acquire it.'

Simone Weil, 1942

References

Abrams, F. (2012) 'Is the new chief inspector of schools just an instrument of government?', *The Guardian* [Online], 23 January. Retrieved from: www.bit.ly/2KIbhVt

Allen, R. (2017) *Making teaching a job worth doing (again)*. Caroline Benn Memorial Lecture [Transcript], 7 November. Retrieved from: www.bit.ly/2RdshTQ

And All That Blog (2016) '"Outstanding" schools and inspection regimes perpetuate shit marking!', [Blog], 16 October. Retrieved from: www.bit.ly/2Nzlx4u

Ashman, G. (2017) 'Understanding the PISA 2015 findings about science teaching', *Filling the Pail* [Blog], 19 March. Retrieved from: www.bit.ly/2VqwJEn

Aubrey, E. (2016) 'It's official: your school's marking policy is probably wrong', *The Guardian* [Online], 29 November. Retrieved from: www.bit.ly/2RMYaD0

Burgess, S. (2014) 'Understanding the success of London's schools', *CMPO Working Paper* 14/333. Bristol: The Centre for Market and Public Organisation, University of Bristol. Retrieved from: www.bit.ly/2Yf32TY

Christodoulou, D. (2017) *Making good progress? The future of assessment for learning*. Oxford: Oxford University Press.

Chu, B. (2017) 'Income gap between people from rich and poor backgrounds has almost doubled, IFS figures reveal', *The Independent* [Online], 11 August. Retrieved from: www.bit.ly/326m55j

Curtis, P. (2009) 'Ofsted's new mission – to get rid of boring teachers', *The Guardian* [Online], 5 January. Retrieved from: www.bit.ly/2JqfDPJ

Department for Education (2011) *Teachers' standards*. London: The Stationery Office. Retrieved from: www.bit.ly/31zy1fv

Department for Education (2018) *Induction for newly qualified teachers (England)*. London: The Stationery Office. Retrieved from: www.bit.ly/31VG7iQ

Didau, D. (2017a) 'Is growth mindset bollocks?', *David Didau* [Blog], 25 January. Retrieved from: www.bit.ly/2vKyTzl

Didau, D. (2017b) 'What teachers need to know about intelligence – part 2: the effects of education', *David Didau* [Blog], 22 May. Retrieved from: www.bit.ly/2KW1f33

Enser, M. (2017) 'Schools must say "no" to out-of-hours revision sessions, for the collection good of the profession', *Tes* [Online], 10 December. Retrieved from: www.bit. ly/2NrsMM9

Facer, J. (2015) 'At what cost?', *Reading all the Books* [Blog], 28 November. Retrieved from: www.bit.ly/2FJNzUM

Garner, R. (2014) 'What is "the Blob" and why is Michael Gove comparing his enemies to an unbeatable sci-fi mound of goo which once battled Steve McQueen?', *The Independent* [Online], 7 February. Retrieved from: www.bit.ly/2xjHvxK

Garner, R. (2016) 'Number of poor students attending UK's leading universities falls despite millions spent to encourage them to apply', *The Independent* [Online], 18 February. Retrieved from: www.bit.ly/2Xnr5iq

Ghose, T. (2013) 'Why we're all above average', *Live Science* [Website], 6 February. Retrieved from: www.bit.ly/2Je2xpB

Great Britain. *Education (Schools) Act 1992: Elizabeth II. Chapter 38.* (1992) London: The Stationery Office. Retrieved from: www.bit.ly/2XIrXm5

Griffin, E. (2014) *Liberty's dawn: a people's history of the industrial revolution.* New Haven, CT: Yale University Press.

Hendrick, C. (2015) 'The McNamara fallacy and the problem with numbers in education', *Chronotope* [Blog], 4 April. Retrieved from: www.bit.ly/2YyuhJz

Henry, J. (2013) 'Teacher "bias" gives better marks to favourite pupils, research reveals', *The Telegraph* [Online], 6 January. Retrieved from: www.bit.ly/2FiERMX

Hutchinson, J. (2016) 'School inspection in England: is there room to improve?', *Education Policy Institute* [Website], 22 November. Retrieved from: www.bit.ly/2YeExq2

Hymas, C. (2018) 'Candidates in up to 40% of A-level and GCSE exams may be awarded incorrect grades, study finds', *The Telegraph* [Online], 30 November. Retrieved from: www.bit.ly/2XheBwz

Independent Teacher Workload Review Group (2016) *Eliminating unnecessary workload around marking.* Department for Education. London: The Stationery Office. Retrieved from: www.bit.ly/3231ZJ5

Kidson, M. and Norris, E. (2014) *Implementing the London challenge.* York: Joseph Rowntree Foundation. Retrieved from: www.bit.ly/2RBdpPo

Kingsnorth, S. (2018) 'SATs are not fit for purpose', *Medium* [Website], 6 January. Retrieved from: www.bit.ly/2MTXNrI

Lemov, D. (2015) 'Are you throwing dollars?', *Teach Like a Champion* [Blog], 28 January. Retrieved from: www.bit.ly/2X0pH4Q

Lynch, S., Mills, B., Theobald, K. and Worth, J. (2017) *Keeping your head: NFER analysis of headteacher retention.* Slough: NFER. Retrieved from: www.bit.ly/2NmC4af

Menzies, L. (2013) 'Do struggling schools improve?', *LKMco* [Website], 6 December. Retrieved from: www.bit.ly/31S2d5X

Merrick, M. (2017) 'Socially mobile?', *Four Thought.* BBC Radio 4, 29 November. Retrieved from: www.bbc.in/2YAwqEg

Newmark, B. (2016) 'We need Maja', *Learning History* [Blog], 1 July. Retrieved from: www.bit.ly/2YewwS5

Newmark, B. (2017) 'Why target grades miss the mark', *Ben Newmark* [Blog], 10 September. Retrieved from: www.bit.ly/30tAdo9

Nye, P. and Rollett, S. (2017) 'How do Ofsted ratings relate to Progress 8 scores?', *FFT Education Datalab* [Website], 11 October. Retrieved from: www.bit.ly/2YbHbgj

Old, A. (2013) 'The Ofsted teaching style', *Scenes from the Battleground* [Blog], 20 May. Retrieved from: www.bit.ly/2V9sE27

Ramesh, R. (2013) 'England's young people near bottom of global league table for basic skills', *The Guardian* [Online], 8 October. Retrieved from: www.bit.ly/2P3w09j

Richardson, H. (2016) 'Many teachers "working 60-hour week"', *BBC News* [Online], 10 October. Retrieved from: www.bbc.in/2JfI80J

Robertson, A. (2017) 'Ofsted wipes academy convertor reports after 5 years', *Schools Week* [Website], 24 October. Retrieved from: www.bit.ly/2J71CVb

Robinson, M. (2019) 'Cultural mobility', *Trivium 21c* [Blog], Retrieved from: www.bit.ly/2JrZ04l

Sims, S. (2016) 'High-stakes accountability and teacher turnover: how do different school inspection judgements affect teachers' decisions to leave their school?', *DoQSS Working Papers* 16-14. London: UCL Department of Quantitative Social Science. Retrieved from: www.bit.ly/2Xa5633

Tressell, R. (2012) *The ragged trousered philanthropists*. Ware: Wordsworth Editions.

Vaughan, R. (2017) 'Schools must stop "mocksted" inspections', *iNews* [Website], 10 March. Retrieved from: www.bit.ly/2Y9A085

Weale, S. (2017) 'Teachers' pay in England down by 12% in 10 years, influential study reveals', *The Guardian* [Online], 12 September. Retrieved from: www.bit.ly/2XiPMwa

Weale, S. (2018) 'Young adults most pessimistic on UK social mobility – poll', *The Guardian* [Online], 11 December. Retrieved from: www.bit.ly/2XkTiX3

Weil, S. (2012) 'Reflections on the right use of school studies with a view to the love of God', *Hagia Sophia Classical Academy* [Website]. Retrieved from: www.bit.ly/2Lvqx7Q

Worth, J., De Lazzari, G. and Hillary, J. (2017) *Teacher retention and turnover research*. Slough: NFER. Retrieved from: www.bit.ly/30jxTzD